Praise for

# *SPIRIT MEANS BUSINESS*

"*Spirit Means Business* is as fun to read as it is enlightening—essential reading for anyone committed to success in their personal and financial lives. Alan reminds us that we can both achieve the things that we want and be our authentic selves. The wisdom he has gathered from his own life experiences is the real deal."

— **Ken Honda**, Japan's all-time best-selling business author

"*Spirit Means Business* teaches us that our desire for spiritual evolution and business success are not in conflict with one another. As Alan Cohen beautifully reminds us, they're linked in a powerful way."

— **Mike Robbins**, author of *Bring Your Whole Self to Work*

"I love this book! Alan Cohen has gotten inside our heads, exposing that the illusions we've learned to relate to as truth about money, sacrifice, and success aren't rooted in reality at all! *Spirit Means Business* is a powerful and practical guide through the maze of these myths, providing a path to prosperity with integrity at the core."

— **Nancy Levin**, author of *Worthy: Boost Your Self-Worth to Grow Your Net Worth*

"Alan Cohen is one of my favorite teachers. He somehow manages to be both super mellow *and* super no-nonsense intense. In *Spirit Means Business* he helps us achieve what we all really want: how to prosper wildly (!) without selling our souls. I loved the book and highly recommend it—especially if you've wondered how to integrate your spirituality and your ambition. I believe the world needs more of us spiritually minded people to become *much* more economically empowered so we can change the world together. I think this book is a great resource for the movement."

— **Brian Johnson**, CEO of Optimize and
creator of *Philosophers' Notes*

"In *Spirit Means Business*, Alan Cohen dispels the myths of hardship commonly associated with professional advancement and awakens the reader to an alternate reality where the air is fresher, the colors more brilliant, and the money flows. As an entrepreneur and business coach, who transformed from working very hard to succeeding with ease, I highly recommend this insightful book. It is a blessing for any entrepreneur or professional who feels the call for greater joy, passion, and profitability in their business. Listen to his immense wisdom, self-examine with his lessons, and watch your life become lighter and more joyful and for you to prosper with greater ease."

— **Roberta Ross**, president of www.SixFigureRealEstateCoach.com
and host of *Free Yourself to Success Podcast*

# SPIRIT MEANS BUSINESS

## ALSO BY ALAN COHEN

*Are You as Happy as Your Dog?*

*A Course in Miracles Made Easy\**

*Dare to Be Yourself*

*A Deep Breath of Life\**

*A Daily Dose of Sanity\**

*Don't Get Lucky, Get Smart*

*The Dragon Doesn't Live Here Anymore*

*Enough Already\**

*The Grace Factor*

*Handle with Prayer\**

*Happily Even After\**

*Have You Hugged a Monster Today?*

*I Had It All the Time*

*How Good Can It Get?*

*Joy Is My Compass\**

*Lifestyles of the Rich in Spirit\**

*Linden's Last Life\**

*Looking In for Number One*

*My Father's Voice*

*The Peace That You Seek*

*Relax into Wealth*

*Rising in Love\**

*Setting the Seen*

*The Tao Made Easy\**

*Why Your Life Sucks and What You Can Do about It*

*Wisdom of the Heart\**

\*Available from Hay House

❊   ❊   ❊

Please visit:

Hay House UK: www.hayhouse.co.uk
Hay House USA: www.hayhouse.com®
Hay House Australia: www.hayhouse.com.au
Hay House India: www.hayhouse.co.in

# SPIRIT MEANS BUSINESS

## THE WAY TO PROSPER WILDLY WITHOUT SELLING YOUR SOUL

### ALAN COHEN

**HAY HOUSE**

Carlsbad, California • New York City
London • Sydney • New Delhi

**Published in the United Kingdom by:**
Hay House UK Ltd, Astley House, 33 Notting Hill Gate, London W11 3JQ
Tel: +44 (0)20 3675 2450; Fax: +44 (0)20 3675 2451; www.hayhouse.co.uk

**Published in the United States of America by:**
Hay House Inc., PO Box 5100, Carlsbad, CA 92018-5100
Tel: (1) 760 431 7695 or (800) 654 5126
Fax: (1) 760 431 6948 or (800) 650 5115; www.hayhouse.com

**Published in Australia by:**
Hay House Australia Ltd, 18/36 Ralph St, Alexandria NSW 2015
Tel: (61) 2 9669 4299; Fax: (61) 2 9669 4144; www.hayhouse.com.au

**Published in India by:**
Hay House Publishers India, Muskaan Complex, Plot No.3, B-2,
Vasant Kunj, New Delhi 110 070
Tel: (91) 11 4176 1620; Fax: (91) 11 4176 1630; www.hayhouse.co.in

Text © Alan Cohen, 2019

The moral rights of the author have been asserted.

The information given in this book should not be treated as a substitute for professional medical advice; always consult a medical practitioner. Any use of information in this book is at the reader's discretion and risk. Neither the author nor the publisher can be held responsible for any loss, claim or damage arising out of the use, or misuse, of the suggestions made, the failure to take medical advice or for any material on third-party websites.

A catalogue record for this book is available from the British Library.

Tradepaper ISBN: 978-1-78180-844-3
E-book ISBN: 978-1-4019-5337-9

Cover design: Brad@Foltzdesign.com • Interior design: Bryn Starr Best

Printed and bound by CPI Group (UK) Ltd, Croydon, CR0 4YY

*To Ken Honda, whose generosity of spirit*
*has taught me that kindness*
*is the heart of success*

# CONTENTS

INTRODUCTION • xi

A FEW NOTES TO THE READER • xvii

ILLUSION #1:      Success Demands Suffering • 1

ILLUSION #2:      The Answers You Seek Are Somewhere Out There • 25

ILLUSION #3:      Your Success Depends on External Conditions • 45

ILLUSION #4:      Your Supply Is Limited • 63

ILLUSION #5:      You Must Earn Your Good • 87

ILLUSION #6:      The Goal of Work Is Money • 107

ILLUSION #7:      To Succeed, Get as Much as You Can While Giving as Little as You Can • 131

ILLUSION #8:      Competition Is Healthy and Required • 155

ILLUSION #9:      The Rules of Business Are an Exception to the Laws of Life • 179

ILLUSION #10:     You Must Sacrifice Your Life for Work • 203

EPILOGUE • 229

ACKNOWLEDGMENTS • 231

ABOUT THE AUTHOR • 233

THE GREAT ENEMY OF THE TRUTH IS VERY OFTEN NOT THE LIE—
DELIBERATE, CONTRIVED, AND DISHONEST—
BUT THE MYTH—
PERSISTENT, PERSUASIVE, AND UNREALISTIC.

– John F. Kennedy

# INTRODUCTION

Not very long ago, people believed all kinds of things that seem unbelievable, even ridiculous, now. Until the end of the 19th century, doctors attempted to cure illnesses by draining nearly all the blood from a patient's body. Half of the United States fought for the right to own slaves. Into the early 20th century, heroin was sold over the counter in corner drugstores as "a perfect guardian of health," and Bayer marketed the substance as an aspirin for children. Women's magazines urged the reader to wake up an hour before her husband and apply makeup so she would look beautiful when he opened his eyes. As recently as the 1950s, some doctors performed lobotomies by jamming an ice pick into the eye sockets of mentally ill patients. The vice president of Planned Parenthood advised pregnant women to smoke as a treatment for constipation. To this day, the Flat Earth Society argues vehemently that the earth is a disk and if you cruise over its edge, you will fall into the abyss. Only recently have we begun to emerge from the Dark Ages, and in many ways we have yet to do so. Yet there are people who are more committed to advancing their lives than remaining asleep. Irish writer Stopford Brooke urged, "If a thousand old beliefs were ruined in our march to truth, we must still march on."

One of the areas begging sorely for our awakening is the arena of business and money. As advanced as we are in commerce, many of us still subscribe to limiting fear-based ideas and attitudes that keep us from thriving. Over many years coaching and training thousands of clients to forge new paths to success in business, I have found three groups of people who struggle with their money and their jobs.

The first group is earning a decent income from their corporate positions, but their souls are starving. My client Sara is a computer graphic designer for a major motion picture studio. She told me, "At first I was excited about the job, but over time my company has become more corporate and less humane. My job has become more and more rote, to the point that I feel more like a machine than a person. Management keeps piling on more tasks with shorter deadlines. They give generous bonuses when a film is successful, but the more they pay, the more they expect. They think they own me, and my work spills into evenings and weekends. My social life has shriveled to a nub. I feel tired and achy and I don't want to get out of bed in the morning. I wish I could just quit and do something more life-giving; I fantasize about working for a company with better values, or starting my own business. But I have lots of bills to pay, and the idea of starting my own business or reinventing myself feels daunting. I am not happy here, but at least I can count on a paycheck."

My client Tom speaks for another group: entrepreneurs who have remained true to their passion but feel overwhelmed with the tasks of running a business and hustling to generate income. "When I got my degree as a psychotherapist, I didn't want to work for an institution, so I set up a private practice. I love my connections with my clients; I find it supremely rewarding to help people get out of distress and live happier, more productive lives. But the bureaucratic element is killing me. To get paid by insurance, I must document all the details of my interactions with clients, so I sit with a computer between us, taking notes rather than looking them in the eye. The follow-up paperwork is unbelievably time-consuming. I spend one-third of my time seeing patients and two-thirds filing reports. Add to that the tasks of advertising, maintaining a website, supervising a few staff members, paying taxes, and all the other requirements to manage a business. I feel almost defeated. When I go home at night, I think, 'I can't believe this is how I was born to work and live.'"

There is one other group I regularly encounter, represented by my client Sonya, an artist. "I don't care about making a lot of money; I would prefer not to have to even deal with it. I would paint all day if I could. My greatest joy is in expressing myself and sharing my creations with others. When I'm in my studio, time and the world disappear. It makes my heart sing to know that I am bringing more beauty to the world. But when I walk out, I am faced with my rent, auto payments, and other bills. I am embarrassed to admit how much time I spend juggling credit cards, grabbing the latest intro promotion, and borrowing from one card to offset another. I wish I could be supported by my artwork, but I haven't been. I had to take a waitress job to get my bills paid. By the time I get home I'm beat and my energy for art is depleted. I feel like a sellout."

As I have come to know these clients and the groups they represent, I realize they are a lot more alike than different. They have all gotten out of balance and failed to integrate their inner life and their material world. Somewhere in their minds there is a split between money and passion, between worldly success and soul reward. One group works for money but has lost their soul. Another group has remained true to their passion and functions well in the marketplace, but the daily grind has eclipsed their joy. The third group doesn't care about money, but they have to deal with it. This group is thriving spiritually but malnourished materially. Members of each group have a piece of the puzzle, but do not see the larger picture into which their piece fits. They don't believe they can have it all, so they settle for what they have and still feel empty.

We are not doomed to be caught, like children of a divorce, in the chasm between passion and material reward. The seemingly disparate worlds can be bridged. The challenges we face at work are not punishments, curses, or impassable obstacles. They are opportunities to discover where we are limiting ourselves and how we can grow beyond those perceived limitations. They point us to where we have gotten out of balance so we can restore it. You *can* get paid well for doing what you love and enjoy a thriving personal life as well. It is my intention in this book to help you do just that.

I am qualified to map this path because I have struggled with the same issues you may be facing. Many years ago I wrote a book, *The Dragon Doesn't Live Here Anymore*, for the sheer joy of creative self-expression. I couldn't find a publisher to print it, so I published it myself with my mother's life savings. To my surprise, the book caught on by word of mouth and became a bestseller. Before long I was jaunting around the globe presenting lectures to thousands of people and selling books by the case, generating huge checks for more money than I knew what to do with. I had to set up some structure to manage my activities, and suddenly I was thrust into the business world. In spite of my desire to just write books and teach seminars, I had to establish a corporation, negotiate contracts, do spreadsheets, set up marketing campaigns, maintain a certain income to pay my mortgage, make detailed travel arrangements, hire and fire employees, wade through recessions, pay taxes and insurance, and all the other accoutrements that come with being a business owner in today's convoluted world. If I delegated some of those tasks, I had to manage the people to whom I delegated, which was a job in itself. Of sheer necessity I had to learn how to handle all of those details, deliver quality products and services to my customers, and still have a life besides work. Now, some 35 years later, I realize that the tasks of business I so vehemently resisted provided some of the most powerful transformational lessons of my lifetime. While business has been a demanding taskmaster, it has also been a sterling teacher and a dynamic liberator. Although I would rather have sat in the woods writing books, the spiritual insights I gained from learning to work in the marketplace have empowered me far more than simply writing. Those insights have, in fact, made me a better writer and teacher. It is said, "What's in the way *is* the way."

If your world of business and finance seems to be in the way for you, I would like to show you how it *is* the way. How you can make the workplace your friend and let it empower you rather than debilitate you. This is a book about wise investment strategies. Not stock market investments; there are plenty of good books that can help you with that. This is a book about investing in yourself, the most valuable commodity you will ever handle—and ultimately the most profitable. Whether you are a corporate worker, an entrepreneur, a creative spirit, or simply looking for a more effective way to integrate your money with your life, the journey we are about to take will help you recognize your inherent worthiness and expand your field of vision to create space for inner and outer riches. While your job and the money you handle are ostensibly about your vocational journey, they are more fundamentally about the journey of your soul.

The first step to removing any obstacle is to discover and dismantle the beliefs that are keeping you stuck. Where are you denying your aliveness? What do you believe you have to do first before you can do what you really want to do? Who or what seems to be limiting your income? If you experience any struggle, strife, or lack in your livelihood, you must believe some lie. Truth does not require sacrifice; only fear, the enemy of joy, demands suffering. Every fear masks a truth that, when unearthed, liberates massive earning potential. Working harder will not erase false beliefs, but only reinforce them. Only the spotlight of courageous honesty will dissolve what entraps and reveal your authentic prosperous path.

In the pages that follow, I will identify the ten fundamental illusions that keep you from experiencing deep joy and solid success in your work, and replace them with life-giving principles and practices. I will explain why you may have settled for less than what you really want and motivate you to settle for more. If you are already successful, we will look at ways for you to rise to your next rung of empowerment. If you associate money with fear, I will show you how to make money your servant rather than your master. We will take our power back from beliefs in struggle, dependence on external conditions, the burden to earn, competing in a field of limited supply, allowing work to become a substitute for life, and much more. This book is about freedom from vocational and spiritual bondage. Each chapter contains key principles, real-life stories demonstrating how to apply them, and one or more exercises you can use to activate the skills in your livelihood. These ideas are simple and they work. We are going to apply dynamic truths to your daily life so you see tangible, experiential results. I don't just want you to just think prosperity. I want you to *live* it.

*Spirit Means Business* is a triple entendre. On one level, it means that Higher Power is the source of prosperity. As you align with universal principles, everything you need will come to you. The Creator wants you to be wealthy in every way and will gladly help you achieve all the material success you need. Infinite supply, not the stock market, is the source of your good. On another level, even if you do not believe in a Higher Power, the spirit in which you conduct your work carves the difference between success and failure. Optimistic, upbeat people soar above the crowd, no matter their religious beliefs. Finally, this title affirms that Higher Power is uncompromisingly serious about getting things done. Universal laws always work when you work them. Deny them, and you flounder. A Broadway play sported the title, *Your Arms Too Short to Box with God.* Yet if you knew that the universe is always working on your behalf, why would you want to fight it? To box with God is to fight yourself. When you drop your gloves, doors open.

If you are going to create a new kind of success, you must create more space in your mind to accommodate it. You cannot keep thinking about your career and money in the same way and get a different result. Einstein explained that you cannot solve a problem with the same mind that created it. If you think that the way business is, is the only way it can be, you have painted yourself into a dark corner. If, however, you entertain even a little willingness to rethink how you have been approaching your livelihood, we can work miracles together.

If the universe were random, we would all be in trouble. But life is founded on rock solid truths that make our journey both joyful and successful when we apply them. With universal laws at your back, you are established in certainty and power that anxiety-based striving cannot sustain. Money and passion become inseparable. We are about to cross the bridge from soul-expression to success. When you do, you will have access to both worlds because you realize they are the same.

# A FEW NOTES TO THE READER

The principles in this book are based on a holistic foundation, recognizing that our lives represent the integration of mind, body, and spirit. Each of us has our own idea of who or what that spirit is, how it works, and our relationship to it. I use the terms "Spirit," "Higher Power," "God," "Source," "the universe," and other similar expressions. If you prefer one term over another, feel free to use whatever works for you, or substitute your own valued idea. The Power I refer to is not hung up on what you call it. What is important is that you create a relationship with it that works for you.

I often refer to *A Course in Miracles*, a self-study system of healing, or, as some call it, "spiritual psychotherapy." I have practiced the Course for many years and have a great respect for the positive changes it has brought about in my life and the lives of many others. To explore *A Course in Miracles*, visit www.acim.org.

In some of the anecdotes I recount, I have altered the names of the people described, to honor their privacy. Some of the stories represent an amalgamation of several different experiences, for the sake of brevity and to underscore a principle.

I alternate between using the pronouns "he" and "she" to honor both genders.

# ILLUSION #1:
# SUCCESS DEMANDS SUFFERING

The worlds of business and money are so infiltrated with false beliefs that we hardly see them clearly at all. For many people, business is a battleground, a daily fight for survival riddled with brutal competition. People fight over money, steal, murder, abscond with their employees' life savings, worship money as a god, and condemn it as a devil. Money is the number one cause of arguments among married couples. Nations wage economic-based wars that send thousands of our sons and daughters to their graves. We spend the greater part of our waking hours striving for money, and then we look back on our lives and wish we had taken more time with the people we love. We are in pain because we engage in archaic beliefs and practices as outdated and impractical as a modern executive coming to work wearing a suit of knight's armor. Tragically, for many, business and money form the house of hell.

None of this insanity need be. If we understood what business and money really are and how they are meant to be used, our relationship with them would transform and they would become a source of joy and empowerment rather than survival, divisiveness, and warfare. Any fear, stress, or pain you experience in your work is an arrow pointing you to a darkened area of your mind calling for healing. The answer to your career and financial challenges is not to work harder, quit, or take another loan; it is to revisit your beliefs about money and shift them so you develop wealth from the inside out. In this book we will achieve an *explosive reframe* about money and business, so you see them in a new and empowering light.

The first limiting belief we will address, perhaps the most pervasive and debilitating, is that you must suffer in order to succeed. Genuine achievement, we have been taught by word and model, is attained only by way of struggle, strain, and sacrifice. Our parents, teachers, preachers, and history books point to countless examples of individuals who have toiled and agonized to get where they are. Abraham Lincoln walked three miles after work to return six cents he had mistakenly overcharged a customer. Thomas Edison went through 10,000 failed experiments en route to the incandescent light. Henry Ford weathered two bankruptcies before he established his successful auto company. J. K. Rowling was divorced and penniless, a single mother on welfare, stealing diapers from maternity stores, as a prelude to becoming richer than the Queen of England through her *Harry Potter* series. While we must honor, appreciate, and learn from anyone who courageously overcomes adversity, we don't want to set up our minds so that hardship is always a prerequisite for success. Ease, flow, and joy can take us to the same place, sometimes faster. If you have a hard time believing this, you can see how deeply our programming to suffer has been instilled.

While our teachers and parents often remind us of and even romanticize people who have struggled their way to the top, they do not explain the decisive role that beliefs play in achievement. Those who believe that suffering is a prerequisite for success will suffer and they will succeed. Not because struggle is required, but because all beliefs are self-reinforcing. We don't believe what we prove. We prove what we believe.

Are there really people who achieve big success without struggle? If so, how do they do it? Are you, too, capable of getting where you want to go without getting fried before you arrive? Here are some crucial tips to lighten your journey:

## SEVEN KEYS TO A VASTER ROOM

### 1. Reframe struggle as an arrow pointing you elsewhere.

If something you are doing is not working, doing more of it will not work better. When you get tired of banging your head against a wall, you will look for a door. One afternoon a little bird flew into our living room through an open sliding door. The bird kept fluttering around the ceiling, occasionally landing on a high ledge. We opened all the doors and windows, shooed the tiny creature with a broom, tried to capture it with a net, and sent it psychic messages saying, "Flying around the ceiling and bumping into walls isn't working. Please try something different." But none of our attempts worked. The distraught little creature didn't understand that it had to just dip down a few feet to find its way to freedom. This drama went on until dark, when we left the bird to sleep on the ledge overnight. When we awoke in the morning the bird was chirping loudly, indicating it was quite hungry. We tried some more tactics, still to no avail. Finally we decided to just trust that the bird would somehow find its way out, and we left the house for a while. When we came back the bird was gone.

In some ways all of us are like the bird who was stuck on one way of solving its problem, a way that didn't work. It took strong motivation—hunger—for the bird to seek and find an alternate route that worked. When we become tired of hitting obstacles, struggling with our work and money, we grow so hungry for relief that we ask, "Is there another way out?" Then we find the door to freedom.

Pain pushes and vision pulls. Pain is screaming at you, "This can't be it!" If you were raised in a religion, family, or culture that glorified suffering and sacrifice, you may tend to choose the path of the martyr. But there is nothing holy about self-induced torture. Contrary to what you have been taught, God does not take joy in your pain. Higher Power wants you to be happy. When you refuse to accept struggle as a necessary element of your work and your life, it will diminish and disappear. Drama is a choice. So is ease.

The practical metaphysical teacher Florence Scovel Shinn told her clients, "Struggle to get, struggle to keep." If you have to fight and manipulate to obtain something, you will have to fight and manipulate to keep it. Many people in rocky relationships believe that once they get married, smooth sailing will follow. Or "when we have a baby our relationship will become stable." Then they discover that a ring on a finger, a marriage certificate, or a child does not make a marriage. The attitudes and actions of the partners steer the relationship. Unless you change the mind-set that created a rocky relationship before marriage, you will continue the rough ride. Likewise, if you are wrestling with someone to make a deal, you will probably wrestle with the results of that deal, and if you have an ongoing relationship with that individual, the wrestling match will go on. Struggle perpetuates itself until you choose otherwise.

If at first you don't succeed, redefine success. My client Sara was considering enrolling in a graduate program to get an advanced degree in her medical profession. Then a pizza delivery guy showed up at Sara's door wearing a T-shirt displaying the logo of the college she wanted to attend. She took this as a sign that she was on the right track, and she submitted her application.

To Sara's surprise, she was not accepted. Disappointed and confused, she asked me, "Why did I get that sign if I was not supposed to enroll in that program?"

"How much did you really want to get into that program?" I asked her.

Sara gave my question some thought, and told me, "To be honest, I feel bored doing the same kind of work over many years. Truth be told, I would prefer to work in holistic or alternative medicine rather than a traditional model." The more Sara and I discussed this new direction, the more passion she displayed.

"Still, then, why did that guy show up wearing that T-shirt?" she asked.

"You saw that logo not because you were supposed to go to that college," I suggested. "You saw it to stimulate your process of applying, getting rejected, and introspecting to get clear on what you would rather do instead."

While Sara initially believed that not being accepted to that program was a sign of failure, it was one element in a broader success. She was not being rejected. She was being redirected.

Success and failure are interpretations, not facts. What appears to be a huge success can prove to be a major distraction and turn into a nightmare. What appears to be a huge failure can serve as brilliant guidance to learn something crucial and lead you to an even more meaningful success. Be careful what you call a failure. The universe is guiding you more than you know.

---

## THE MYTH:

Struggle means you are getting somewhere.

## THE REALITY:

Struggle means you are being directed elsewhere.

---

## 2. Burn with the fire of purpose.

When your intention is strong, obstacles that would stop people with weaker intention will not thwart you. My friend Gudrun Cable, an appreciator of great literature, wanted to create a hotel with rooms decorated according to the lives and themes of famous writers. She found a perfect hotel for sale on the windswept Oregon coast and applied for a loan to purchase it. Gudrun was turned down again and again and again. She applied to 30 lenders for loans until one finally agreed. Then she gathered a group of her friends to help decorate the rooms, each in the style of a particular author like Mark Twain, Edgar Allen Poe, and Dr. Seuss. Today the Sylvia Beach Hotel is a booming success, offering one of the most unique lodging and retreat experiences in the world. Gudrun's intention to create that hotel was stronger than any of the lenders' intentions to deny her, so she succeeded because she burned with the fire of purpose.

When an aspiring writer asked Ernest Hemingway if he should take up writing, Hemingway answered, "If anything can stop you, let it." When a young woman asked Barbra Streisand if she should pursue a singing career, Streisand told her, "If you have to ask, don't." If something can keep you from doing what you love, you don't really love it. When passion is your prime motivator, nothing will be able to stop you from claiming your destiny.

You might argue that Gudrun Cable's journey to obtain her hotel was a struggle to surmount the hurdles before her. That is so only at the surface level of appearances. On a deeper level, she was on an exciting adventure, the joy of which far exceeded any sense of struggle. Struggle is not a circumstance; it is a state of mind. Refuse to participate in mental and emotional struggle, and authentic passion will fuel you to reach your goal.

---

### THE MYTH:
Obstacles have the power to stop
you and turn you back.

### THE REALITY:
When you're burning with the fire of purpose,
challenges cease to be obstacles and become fuel.

---

## 3. Partner with Higher Power.

If you think you have to go it alone and do it all yourself, you will bear a heavy self-fabricated cross. Even if you succeed as an ego, you will fail as a spirit. You may close the deal, win the award, or obtain the position, but if your soul is battered or starving, what good are the medals? If you are hell-bent on marching as an army of one, you will engender conflicts, keep facing the next uphill battle, and get sick. Some of the highest-profile people are the most miserable. They are worldly successes but spiritual failures. If you believe that everything depends on you, you will grow weary and be crushed. But if you allow a Higher Power to guide your business, your burden will be lightened and all you need will come to you. Authentic achievement is a co-creation. Do your part and Spirit will do its part.

When I write a book, I never feel that I am writing it by myself. The content is being given to me by a greater source. My job is to listen carefully and deliver the material to the world as true to its intent as possible. The book has already been written and I am the recording secretary. I never struggle to squeeze material forth. My role is to quiet my mind and open the door. What comes through that door amazes me! The experience is simultaneously humbling and empowering. Source has never failed me, and it will not fail you.

Most creative people report a similar experience. Nikola Tesla, the genius visionary who advanced society immeasurably with his astounding inventions, reported that his ideas came to him in a flash. His job was to flesh them out. World-changing ideas are not sourced by people. They are sourced by God. But God needs us to bring those ideas to life. That is how valuable and trustworthy you are, and how important is your role as a co-creator of magnificent productions.

---

## THE MYTH:
You have to do it all alone.

## THE REALITY:
Higher Power is eager, willing, and able to
help you and work through you.

---

## 4. Let the Law of Matching guide you.

When I rented a car, the agent gave me the key and told me my vehicle was in stall 307. I walked to that stall, pressed the "open trunk" button, and nothing happened. I tried a few more times, and still the trunk remained closed. Then I looked down the row of cars and saw that the trunk of the car in stall 303 had opened. I went to that car, which responded to all of my button commands. That was my car. No matter what erroneous stall number the agent had given me, the frequency of that button control was a match to that car. Likewise, when you broadcast the frequency of your authentic self and your pure intentions, everything that matches your broadcast will make itself known and available to you.

You own what you own, whether it's a job, house, or relationship, because it belongs to you by *right of your consciousness*. What is yours is yours because it is a match to who you are. Mean-spirited people, foolish manipulators, or external changes cannot separate you from your good. Steve Jobs co-founded Apple Computers, innovated a world-changing industry, and made Apple a worldwide household name. Then the company fired him and went into a tailspin almost to bankruptcy. Apple reinstated Jobs at the helm, and the company soared to new heights, eclipsing even big oil corporations as the world's leading earner. Now many of us cannot live without Apple-originated devices that didn't exist a short time ago. Jobs and Apple belonged to each other, and the misguided machinations of others could not thwart that ironclad relationship. If something is a match to your passion, talent, and intentions, it will come to you and stay with you as long as there is purpose in that connection. As poet John Burroughs eloquently affirmed, "What is mine shall know my face."

---

## THE MYTH:

External forces and foolish or unkind people can prevent you from achieving your goals.

## THE REALITY:

The Law of Matching will join you and keep you with your good.

---

## 5. Clearly state your vision, intention, and desires.

Drake is a landscaper who had a number of accounts in an up-scale neighborhood. Then one of his account holders told Drake he wanted to hire him full time. "Tell me what your ideal job is," the owner requested.

Drake went home and wrote out the details of his ideal job: the hours, the crew he would need, the equipment, and the salary. He put the paper aside, and over the next day he realized that what he had written was not exactly his ideal job. It was what he thought he could get; besides, he didn't want to push the owner too hard. Then he remembered that the owner had asked him for his *ideal* situation, not a fear-based compromise.

Drake upgraded several elements of his requirements and again put the paper aside. Later that day he thought of a few more features that would really make the job ideal, and he added them. This process went on until Drake felt that what he had written represented his true vision. He didn't know if the owner would go for any or all of his requests, but at least he was being true to the invitation to state his ideal situation.

Drake then showed the owner the paper listing his ideal requirements. The man looked over the paper, thought for a moment, and replied, "Fine."

The first step to getting what you want is asking for it. Trust that the universe is capable of providing it. Life is unlimited in its capacity to deliver anything you can imagine, and far more. Your needs and talents are registered in the mind of All That Is, as are the needs and talents of everyone and everything that interlaces with your journey. Worldly employment agencies and dating services are but symbolic of the far vaster agency that joins people and situations that belong together.

You may not, of course, have an employer or relationship partner say "Fine" to all of your requests as you present them. Yet one thing is for sure: If you ask for all of what you want, your chances of getting it, or most of it, are far greater than if you ask for none or some or most of what you want. The stronger and clearer your statement of intention, the stronger and clearer the response you will receive.

After you have asked, leave space for the universe to give you something even better, perhaps different from what you have asked for. When you insist from ego, you may set yourself up to miss a superior alternative. Complete your prayer, affirmation, or request with "this or better." You will be amazed at how cleverly the universe knows how to provide for you in ways you could not anticipate.

## ■ ■ ■ MY IDEAL CAREER PATH ■ ■ ■

Take a few moments now to write out your vision of your ideal job, career, or business situation. Note every element of your intention, with as many details as possible. Include only those elements that bring you joy, and none that are obligatory, guilt-induced, compromised, habitual, or have some aspect that is not to your liking. Keep going until you have included every element, even tiny inklings of how good it could get. Don't get hung up trying to figure out how you are going to achieve your goal, and don't let yourself get sidetracked by fear, self-doubt, or a negative history. For this exercise, dwell wholeheartedly in your vision.

When you have finished your list, put aside the document and then revisit it after a day or two. You will probably think of some more attributes. Upgrade your list to match your fuller ideal. Don't mitigate, apologize, or conciliate. State what you would ask for if you were really honest.

Keep revising your list until you are fully satisfied. Take the paper and place it in a Bible, *A Course in Miracles*, this book, or any other book that contains positive promises. Then release your request to the universe, completing with, "And so it is."

You can also use this exercise to manifest any goal outside of business that's important to you—a relationship, living situation, health condition, travel vision, or any other ideal you desire.

Now let the universe work on your behalf. God has heard your request. So have you. Behold an unbeatable combination of intention and the power to manifest it.

### AFFIRM

*I am now open, ready, and willing to receive [_____]*
*or better, easily, joyfully, with help from the universe to manifest*
*what will best serve me and everyone involved.*
*And so it is.*

## 6. Work with the willing.

Intention is the engine that powers creation; it is the crucial factor in manifesting success. Everything that happens is the result of intention. Another name for intention is willingness.

If you are to create success with a team, whether with a partner, a customer, or a large company, the other members of that team must be willing. Nothing is more powerful than shared willingness.

When you attempt to achieve a goal with someone who is not willing, you have a hole in the bucket. It is very difficult to move ahead with someone who harbors weak, mixed, negative, or resistant intentions. If you are getting no results or conflicted results, examine your intentions and the intentions of others involved. Honest inspection will reveal that the problem is often related to low or divided intentions.

Have the courage to confront weak or conflicted intentions within yourself and your team. Some friends of mine used to meet once a week to drive together to attend a seminar series on the theme of integrity. One evening the group piled into one lady's new car, she turned the ignition key, and the car wouldn't start. She tried several times, still no response. The driver turned to the other people in the car and stated, "There is a lie in the space. What is it?" After an awkward silence, a woman in the back seat admitted, "I don't really want to go." The group had a brief discussion about the woman's resistance to attending the seminar, and through the process she dropped her resistance. The driver turned the key again and the car started. Through her training in the seminar series, the driver had learned that when something that should be working is not working, there is some breakdown in the integrity of the person or group involved. Integrity means that the life you are living on the outside is a match to who you are on the inside. When there is a gap between the two, efficiency falters. Bring that breach into the light, heal it, and things will start working again.

Morna Simeona was a well-loved teacher of the Hawaiian healing technique of *ho'oponopono* or "restoring well-being through balance." One day Morna was called to a hospital to consult with the business office, where the accounts receivable department was having ongoing problems with computer malfunctions. Morna interviewed the workers in that department and found that a number of them did not want to continually ask ill people for money. Morna conducted a forgiveness exercise in which she asked the workers to forgive the hospital for requesting those payments; themselves for participating in that task; the patients for not paying; and the computers for not working. (You can see how many elements of resistance were clogging the space.) When the group achieved a level of release, the computers began to work again and remained functional.

Both of the above examples demonstrate the vital relationship between willingness, or its lack, and creating positive results. This is why it is so important to work with the willing as a group, and to find where your own willingness lives and proceed from your true intention.

> # THE MYTH:
> If you just keep pushing ahead in the face of mixed or contrary intentions, you will succeed.
>
> # THE REALITY:
> Clearing mixed intentions and aligning fully with your goal paves the fastest and easiest route to success.

## 7. Self-nurture as you proceed.

My friend David is a very successful attorney with over 40 years of experience. He has earned the respect of his industry and commands significant fees. David told me, "When I get all balled up in a case, I go out to the backyard and do some gardening. That is my therapy. In that space I think more clearly and answers come to me that I didn't get while sitting in the office. When I return to work I am far more effective."

Balance your work with rest, renewal, and activities that feed your soul. You can squeeze a sponge just so much before it dries out and loses its power to clean; at some point it must absorb more water if it is to remain effective. When you have reached a point of diminishing returns, you help no one by pushing on. Joyful activities compose the water that sustains your spirit. Don't hesitate or apologize to step away from work, clear your mind and emotions, and regain perspective. Cultivate acts that lift you: connect with friends you love; walk in nature; play music; get a massage; read a novel; watch an uplifting film; go to dinner at your favorite restaurant; or engage in any endeavor that leaves you feeling better. Self-renewal is one of the key contributions you can make to the quality of your work and the success it yields. Your enhanced well-being is a gift to those you work with, as they will far more enjoy working with someone who is refreshed than burnt out, and be inspired to work with you and generate the highest productivity.

> # THE MYTH:
> Working more, harder, and longer will
> yield the results you desire.
>
> # THE REALITY:
> Renewing your spirit will pave the
> way to the results you desire.

## OPEN THE GATES

The tips we have just covered highlight the most direct ways you can rise beyond struggle and create greater ease with your money and your livelihood. Now it's time to address some of the less obvious places where you may be getting logjammed. Situations in which you struggle in the world always reflect situations in which you struggle in your mind. Let's peer more deeply into what's going on inside you that may be blocking your flow of riches, so we can clear the runway for greater wealth to reach you.

There are two gates at which money transactions get jammed. The first and most obvious gate is the one at which you pay money. People with fear related to money become tightfisted and resist paying for commodities and services, even necessary ones.

The more crucial gate we need to open is the resistance to receive money. The amount of money you receive has little to do with the economy, your company, or your customers. Those are the most superficial levels of financial circulation. The key factor in how much money you receive is *your openness to receive it*. This depends on two elements: (1) Your beliefs about supply; and (2) Your sense of worthiness. Both, we will see, are sides of the same coin.If you believe you live in a world of limited supply, you will crimp the pipe through which the universe can pour your good to you. While life is capable of supplying you with all you need, a limiting belief can pinch off a huge flow. One day I noticed that my kitchen faucet was not dispensing water to the sink; the stream was reduced to just a few drops. When a plumber opened up the apparatus, he found that a tiny stone had gotten lodged at a crucial juncture in the stream. While millions of gallons of water were available, the flow was reduced to a trickle because of one little stone. When the plumber removed the stone, the faucet was restored to maximum delivery. Even a small belief in limits can stand between you and the enormous resources available to you. When you remove the stone, you have access to all you need, and more.

Your sense of worthiness is even more crucial than your beliefs about supply. Actually, they are the same: If you know you are enough, you know that the universe can supply enough. If you do not believe you deserve to receive the wealth you desire, you will keep supply at a distance. When students apply for my Life Coach Training Program, I ask them, "What fears or concerns do you have about becoming a life coach?" Most applicants voice some self-doubt: "Who am I to coach other people? I have my own issues I am working on. No one will want to pay me." In the program I explain to the students that those statements issue from a sense of "fraud guilt" from which most people suffer. The belief "I am a phony" is debilitating and can undermine success if left unchecked and unhealed. Even some very successful people believe they are phonies. A survey asked Hollywood movie studio CEOs, "What do you fear the most?" The most common answer was, "I fear that people will discover that I don't really know what I am doing." Meanwhile these CEOs were doing masterful jobs making many millions of dollars for their companies. They just *thought* they were phonies.

A cute story from the video series *The Beatles Anthology* illustrates this very dynamic. At the height of the Beatles' illustrious career, Ringo Starr had a bout with fraud guilt and decided he wasn't fit to be in a band as talented as the Beatles. He went to John Lennon and told him, "I'm leaving the group because I'm not playing well and I feel unloved and out of it, and you three are really close." John replied, "I thought it was you three!" Then

Ringo told Paul McCartney he felt like an outsider. Paul replied, "I thought it was you three!" By that time Ringo's anxieties were assuaged, so he didn't bother going to George Harrison, who might have given a similar reply. The idea that any of these four—Ringo, John, Paul, or George—was not a "real" Beatle seems laughable and ludicrous, since each of those musicians was talented in his own way, and their unique synergy made the Beatles the most successful entertainers in history. But each of them had to face and deal with his own demons. If even the Beatles suffered fraud guilt, you can see what a liar that voice is, and why you should give it no credence and not let it stop you on your own path to success.

## REDEFINE MONEY IN YOUR FAVOR

You have been taught that "money is the root of all evil." Money is *not* the root of all evil. *Fear* is the root of all evil. When fear is applied to money, money becomes a tool of evil. But when trust, mutual support, and generosity are applied to money, it becomes the root of all good.

My friend Charley Thweatt (musicangel.com) wrote a clever song that begins with the lyric, "Why does it feel funny when we talk about money and communication gets weird?" You might be having an altogether pleasant conversation with a friend, spouse, or business associate, until the subject of money comes up. Suddenly solar plexuses clench, tension arises, and defenses come forth. There is not anything inherently tension-inducing about money; like all things, it is a neutral object that we make what we will by projecting our beliefs onto it. If you get uptight when dealing with money, you are being directed toward a limiting belief you are holding about it, and you can heal it. Thus, upsets about money cease to be vexations and instead become golden arrows pointing to transformation by peeling away painful illusions and revealing the truth they have hidden.

One prevalent definition of money in our culture is that it is something to fight over. Money, as I mentioned, is the most frequent subject of arguments among couples. If money is an issue for you, where did you learn to associate it with conflict? Perhaps your family struggled with money when you were a child, or your parents fought over it, or your grandparent survived the Depression or a war and became inordinately frugal as a result, or your mother begrudgingly gave you money to buy a candy bar, or your parents denied themselves vacations or a new car because they had a strong work ethic and believed that self-nurturing was indulgent; or . . . or . . . or . . .

You were not born with negative associations about money. They were *all* learned. Your "core" programming is not core at all. Your true core runs far deeper than social imprinting. Your real self remains perfectly, eternally connected to your Source, which is loving, abundant, and generous. So your journey to greater prosperity is not about traveling to a foreign shore. It is a journey home to your true self.

To begin reclaiming your inherent well-deserved wealth, redefine money as an avenue and expression of positive energy. When you give money, you are giving life. When you receive money, you are receiving love. When money flows through the economy, happiness is circulated and multiplied. Money is a healthy, worthwhile, joy-inducing commodity to have and share. All money transactions are statements of gratitude, mutual support, and unlimited prosperity.

Now that feels a lot better than "money is the root of all evil," doesn't it? Evil minds see evil money while loving minds see loving money. Even more than money lives in your checkbook, it lives in your mind. This explains why all changes in your world of money begin with changes in your mind. Here is my favorite affirmation about money, which some people write or have printed on their checks:

> *Every dollar I spend enriches the economy,*
> *blesses everyone it touches, and returns to me multiplied.*

Now let's take an important step to redefining money in your favor.

## MONEY AS AN INSTRUMENT OF LIFE

Identify a financial transaction in which you feel troubled to pay a person or company:

_____

_____

_____

Reframe and fill in the blanks with the name of the person or company involved in the transaction:

*When I pay [name of person or company], I am giving [name of person or company] life. When I give life, it flows through me and I benefit.*

Identify a financial transaction in which you feel guilty about asking for payment or receiving it:

_____

_____

_____

*REFRAME:*

*When [name of person or company] pays me, [name of person or company] is giving me love. In that transaction, we both benefit.*

Identify a product or service you would like to purchase but have been hesitating:

_____

_____

*REFRAME:*

*When I purchase [name of product or service] for myself, I am giving myself spiritual sustenance and supporting the person or company from which I purchase it.*

### AFFIRM

*I use all financial transactions as
opportunities to circulate love and life.
I benefit along with everyone with whom I interact.*

## SOURCE OR AVENUE?

We impose unnecessary limits on prosperity when we confuse the *avenue* of our sustenance with its *source*. We believe that our well-being depends on a particular person, family, project, company, institution, or government. Then if a family member cuts off our payments, or the deal falls through, or we lose our job, or the government changes its policy, we feel abandoned, vulnerable, or betrayed. If you worry about such a situation, or have experienced it, remember that no person, company, or government is the source of your good. Each is but one of many channels through which providence can find you. The real source of your good is the universe, or life, or God, or however you wish to identify it. One of my favorite *A Course in Miracles* teachings is Lesson 50: *"I am sustained by the love of God."* This lesson asks us to consider the many people and entities we identify as the origin of our providence; then realize they are but channels of prosperity; then take back the power we have attributed to them; and then acknowledge our true Source that extends far beyond any particular avenue through which it flows.

If you resist change or try to force a historical outlet to keep supplying you, you will diminish your returns in two ways: (1) You will shrink your consciousness to a sense of lack, victimization, and battle, and crimp the flow of prosperity; and (2) You will miss noticing other available sources of your good. Miguel de Cervantes's beloved Don Quixote advised, "Look always forward. In last year's nests . . . there are no birds this year." What provided for you yesterday may not be what will provide for you today. Yet rest assured that the Source that took care of you yesterday will take care of you today, tomorrow, and always. "Surely goodness and mercy will follow me all the days of my life . . ."

The Law of Grace that has delivered your blessings will not stop now. The ego is extremely shortsighted, absorbed in pettiness and lack. It sees current negative appearances and extrapolates them to eternity. But if you look back on your life honestly, you will see that you have always been guided and protected. Yes, you have had your challenging moments, but you emerged from them with valuable lessons and enhanced strength. Your good has not ceased and neither will it cease. Life's support for you is unfailing and nonnegotiable. As the saying goes, "God loves you and there's nothing you can do about it."

You can pinch yourself off from the awareness of that love, but your crimping does not remove it. Clouds may momentarily block your view of the sun, but they cannot stop the sun from casting its life-giving rays. Imagine bringing a cloud to the sun itself; the cloud would stand no chance of surviving. It would immediately dissolve. This is precisely what happens when you bring your thoughts of lack and poverty to the Source of all prosperity. Illusions of abandonment dissipate and give way to the reality of providence.

---

## THE MYTH:

A particular job, project, person, family,
company, or organization is the source of your wealth.
If that disappears, you are bereft.

## THE REALITY:

The infinite universe is the source of your wealth.
If one channel of prosperity disappears,
others will appear and support you.

---

## LET THE UNIVERSE TAKE CARE OF THE DETAILS

Higher Power is the invisible hand that orchestrates your success. When you partner with that power, events that would otherwise be painstaking become doable and even easy. Miraculous results unfold that far surpass what you could have engineered by yourself.

My partner, Dee, and I were planning to install an irrigation system on our property to nourish a grove of fruit trees. When we purchased our agricultural parcel, we were not told where the county water line connects to our internal system. We thought we might have to bring in a backhoe to poke around and try to find that connection point, which could have been a long, difficult, and expensive project.

Then we received a phone call from the county water department informing us that their recent meter reading showed a huge spike in our water use, indicating a leak somewhere in our system. In our rural area, our water line runs from our meter over a half mile underground through several neighboring properties. Dee and I had to go out and walk the line to search for the leak. Finally, we found it—precisely at the valve we were looking for as the juncture to hook up our irrigation system! Oddly, that connection point was not even on our property. It was on an adjacent property, ten feet from our border. Even if we had poked around with a backhoe on our property, we would not have found the valve. So the water leak, while it at first appeared to be a nuisance, turned out to be a blessing directing us to the precise point where we needed to look. What brilliant guidance! Then the water department refunded a large portion of the excess cost due to the leak since they have a grace policy for leaks. Many different elements were working together to create a successful result.

Higher Power will likewise organize your good. It is already arranging helpful meetings and events for you, but you may not recognize it. To increase your experience of divine orchestration, look for it, acknowledge it, and celebrate it when it shows up. When you focus on what's working, the universe will send more blessings your way.

## DROP THE STRUGGLE, NOT THE QUEST

Rising above struggle does not imply that you cease to act, become an indolent slacker, wait for your angels to do for you what you can do for yourself, or lie in bed and hope checks float through your window. You will still have to make choices at crucial crossroads, face challenges, and work with diligence and responsibility. You will be required to mobilize courage, perseverance, and strategic action, none of which equal struggle, which is a mind-set more than a condition. Struggle implies that you must battle a force equal to or greater than yourself. But there is no force outside you more powerful than the force within you. You are taller than any hurdle you face. Evil has power only at the shallowest levels of illusion. Penetrate to your Source, and you have access to the might that set the universe in motion and forever oversees it.

How you think about challenges determines whether they will be your enemy or your friend. Reframe challenge as a helper rather than a foe, and regard obstacles as stepping-stones, not roadblocks. What seemed to be a daunting situation becomes enlivening. Walls crumble to reveal opportunity. Hardships turn to blessings. Wisdom disarms adversity by hiring it as an ally.

Successful people are visionaries. They see possibilities beyond what has already been achieved and live in them as if they are already so. You were born into an unenlightened world in order to bring light into the darkness. Throw off the shackles of medieval thinking and leave your suit of armor home. It belongs in a museum, not an office. When you refuse to accept suffering as a prerequisite for success, your career ceases to be a crucifying grind and becomes a liberating adventure.

---

# TRUTH #1
# YOU CAN SUCCEED WITHOUT SUFFERING

---

# ILLUSION #2:
# THE ANSWERS YOU SEEK ARE SOMEWHERE OUT THERE

An ancient parable tells that after the earth was created and humans were about to be placed upon it, a group of gods got together and decided to make life on the planet an adventure. They would hide the secret of life in a unique location and then challenge people to find it. But where to hide it?

"Let's place the secret of life at the top of the highest mountain," one god suggested.

"That won't work," another replied. "People will climb there and find it."

"How about placing the secret of life at the bottom of the sea?" another god offered.

"No, humans will figure out a way to get down there as well."

The council of gods came up with suggestion after suggestion, but each location seemed eventually within the reach of humanity.

Finally, one god lit up and exclaimed, "I've got it! Let's hide the secret of life within each person. They'll *never* think to look there."

So it is with the secret of creating a successful business or career. We tend to believe that we are devoid of wisdom, inept, or unworthy and we must depend on others to tell us how to conduct our livelihood. We then set out on a long quest to gather information from experts who will show us how to succeed.

While we can certainly learn from people with more experience, we cannot afford to give our power away at the expense of our own inner guidance. Absorb the wisdom of those who have mastered their craft, and then integrate it with your own vision and sense of direction. Your inner teacher will guide you very specifically to apply the principles and skills you learn. Don't become a clone of anyone else but instead generate achievement that uniquely belongs to you. People who refuse to do things as they have always been done are the ones who raise the bar for everyone. If you were an employee attending a meeting with Elon Musk[1] at Tesla Motors or SpaceX and you made the point, "That's not the way it has always been done," you would be dismissed from the meeting and possibly your job. Forward thinkers have no tolerance for backward vision.

To improve your life and the world, cast your vision beyond known territory. The maxim of the popular *X-Files* television series is "The truth is out there." This is so in that there are realities that go far beyond what the limited senses show us. Yet ultimately the truth is *in here*. Your inner teacher will tell you all you need to know. All external advancement proceeds from internal awakening. Everyone you meet "out there" reflects a part of you. The division we experience between the inner world and the outer world is fictitious. You are not in the world. The world is in you.

## THE MYTH:

To manage your business and your life,
you must get the advice of experts.

## THE REALITY:

While you can learn from experts, your inner guide will tell you
how to apply what you have learned in a way unique to you.

---

1    You will note that I refer to Elon Musk in this book in a number of different contexts. To me, Musk represents a creative entrepreneur who sincerely seeks to help as many people as possible and improve the quality of life on the planet. No saint, Musk has been criticized for some of his rigorous business practices and his turbulent personal life. Whether or not these critiques are valid, the fact remains that in his short career Musk has moved technological and ecological mountains, and serves as a dynamic and inspiring role model for individuals who wish to put visionary ideas in action to benefit the masses.

## WATCH FOR SIGNS

When you stand at a crossroads, the universe will give you signs. If you are not receiving guidance, it is not because it is not being given. It is because you are not noticing signals when and where they appear. Here are five levels of signs you can use to make wise and productive choices:

## 1. Internal guidance

Internal guidance comes in the form of inklings, hunches, promptings, and urgings. "Out of the blue" you may feel inspired to phone someone about a job, project, or social connection. There may be no apparent reason for this act, but, as the Mazda motto affirmed, "It just feels right." Then you get a result your mind could not have predicted but your soul understands. When Dee and I were searching for a dog to join our family, we found the cutest little puppy in an online ad. I phoned the owner, who told me that the puppy had already been promised to a woman who was to pick him up the next morning. We were so disappointed. The next morning, I had an intuition to phone the owner again, even though she had effectively said no. She informed me that the woman who was supposed to take the puppy had not shown up; if we wanted him, he was ours. We picked him up, immediately fell in love with him, and he has become our most cherished companion, playmate, and inspiration.

It is quite possible to found your life on following inner guidance, and some people do. The more you practice listening to your hunches and acting on them, the more positive results you will observe, and the stronger this vital capacity will become.

The exercise below will help you make and sustain the crucial contact with your Higher Self.

## CONTACTING AND ACTING ON INNER GUIDANCE

*Three business situations in which I am not sure what to do:*

1. _____

2. _____

3. _____

*What my guidance is telling me about each situation:*

1. _____

2. _____

3. _____

*How I would act if I trusted my guidance in these situations* (fill in the "I would" blank with a specific action):

1. *If I trusted my guidance in the situation regarding* _____ ,

*I would* _____ .

2. *If I trusted my guidance in the situation regarding* _____ ,

*I would* _____ .

3. *If I trusted my guidance in the situation regarding* _____ ,

*I would* _____ .

### ▪▪▪ AFFIRM: ▪▪▪

*My inner teacher guides me impeccably.*
*I trust my guidance and I act on it.*

▪ ▪ ▪

## 2. Verbal signs through people

Just as a GPS finds the shortest route to your destination, Spirit will use the most direct pathway to deliver your guidance. Your hint will often come through people, directly or inadvertently. A business associate may tell you, "I am going to a seminar this weekend that I think you would like. Would you care to join me?" Or your supervisor says, "You are not doing very well with marketing, but your web design work is superb. I would like you to shift your focus to design." Or a trusted friend suggests, "You are looking pretty tired lately. I am concerned that you are burning yourself out. I hope you will take some time to renew yourself." God speaks to us through each other. Don't wait for a chorus of angels to descend from heaven playing trumpets and announcing your answer on a big neon sign. More often your answer comes through the normal activities of daily life.

Guidance through people can also come inadvertently. A friend may casually mention that she is taking a course in aromatherapy, for example. When you hear this, something inside you stirs. You feel moved to explore this technique, and as a result your life changes. Or you are listening to a lecture and the speaker mentions a quote by Emerson that answers a question you have been struggling with. Or someone in public says something apparently unrelated to you, but you recognize a message for you. While traveling, Dee and I were studying the teachings of Abraham. In Portland, Oregon, we were staying in a hotel in room 327, and we decided to go to a local auto dealership to look at a car model we had been considering. As we opened the door to the showroom, a voice came over the store's loudspeaker: "Abraham, 327. Please pick up." The dealer's receptionist was summoning a salesman to answer a phone call. We took it as a sign that we were in the right place. We made a good deal on the car and enjoyed it for years.

## THE MYTH:

People and events show up in your world at random.

## THE REALITY:

Every person, encounter, and experience comes to you by an intelligent plan related to your well-being, professional advancement, and spiritual growth.

After I published my book *Are You as Happy as Your Dog?* a Japanese woman living in New York asked me if I would like to have the book published in Japanese. Sure, I told her. I had no idea that this woman had no experience publishing books in any language and no connections with any Japanese publishers. She just thought that Japanese people, who are major dog lovers, would enjoy this lighthearted book. The process of an inexperienced person sending a book to a publisher as a cold call, resulting in the book being published, is quite unusual in any language. Yet the publisher liked the book, printed it, and it went on to become popular in Japan.

Several months later I received an email from Ms. Keiko Anaguchi, director of Dynavision, one of Japan's leading inspirational seminar companies. Keiko had read my book in Japanese and she invited me to present a program in that country. As synchronicity would have it, I was scheduled to take a trip to Bali a few months later, changing planes in Japan. Keiko and I met at the airport and enjoyed a solid connection. My seminar for Dynavision turned out to be a big success, which eventually led me to spend a great deal of time in Japan, working with Japanese clients. My experience with the Japanese people has been one of the most rewarding relationships of my career and my life.

Looking back on how this sequence unfolded, I marvel at how all the elements were orchestrated from the beginning. Spirit used people who were open to what wanted to happen, and it happened. Likewise, you can and will be guided by way of people who are attuned to the intentions and values you hold dear. I also believe in the destiny factor: At a soul level we set up certain important connections and events to foster our growth and success.

(A word of caution: Just because someone makes you an offer or suggests that you do something does not mean you should interpret the act as guidance and automatically accept the offer or follow their advice. Always use discernment and try all invitations and proposals on for size to determine if they resonate with your inner guidance.)

You may also be used as a vehicle to deliver guidance to another person, often unknowingly. In the course of a conversation, you may say something that helps someone, without even trying. I often utter ideas in lectures or coaching that are non sequiturs to the conversation. Sometimes I say things I have never thought of before. The other person lights up and informs me that what I just said is exactly what they needed to hear. The aha! is as surprising to me as it is to the other person. Do not judge or overlook odd or unexpected ideas coming through you. When you are open and willing to be a vessel of service and healing, powerful results will happen through you.

## 3. Nonverbal signs through people

Words represent the smallest element of communication. The far greater portion is nonverbal. Everything in nature communicates impeccably without words, except human beings. It has been said that people invented words in order to lie. Words can lead us to greater truth, but they can also distract us into illusions. Pay attention to what is happening *behind* the words or *instead* of words. People communicate more through what they *don't* say. The Japanese, a culture acutely aware of subtle signals, have a marvelous expression for this faculty: "Read the air."

In my early teens I developed a crush on Donna, a girl next door in the garden apartment complex where we both lived. One day I was sitting with Donna on the stoop between our apartments and I asked her to go out with me on Friday night.

She told me she was busy that night. I asked her about another night, and she was busy for a different reason. I repeated my invitation several times, and for every night I asked her, she said no for a different reason.

When I went back into my apartment, my father told me that he had overheard our conversation and it sounded like the girl just didn't want to go out with me. He suggested that I quit pushing the invitation. Why not turn my attention to someone who did want to date me? Looking back now, I recognize the wisdom of his advice. At the time, I was naïve and I believed that Donna really did have something to do on all those nights she could not see me. If I'd been more astute, I would have read between the lines.

(Thirty-five years later Donna sent me an email saying that she had discovered my work on the Internet. She and her mom later attended my seminar when I came through their city, and we enjoyed a delightful reunion. Ultimately we did have a date—of a different kind than I expected.)

---

## THE MYTH:

You can navigate your business and your life by taking things at face value.

## THE REALITY:

To succeed, you must recognize and respond to communication at subtler levels than the obvious.

---

I learned a similar lesson when I began to work with Japanese business associates. In that culture it is considered impolite to say "no," so people find all kinds of ways to say no without saying it directly. Most commonly they simply do not respond to your email or phone call. Or they will say, "I will think about it," and then do nothing. Or they will make another excuse. After I picked up on this cultural norm, I can now "read the air" better.

*No response is a response.* If you are trying to make a deal, sell something, or strike up a relationship, and the person does not respond, consider their silence a "no." Don't waste your time trying to work with someone who is not equally enthusiastic about working with you. People show up for things they want to do, and they disappear from things they do not want to do. There are other people who want what you have to offer. Quit trying to convince people to do what they are not doing, and instead find someone who recognizes the gift you bring and is eager to receive it.

---

## THE MYTH:

You can succeed by twisting people's arms and convincing or forcing them to do what they do not want to do.

## THE REALITY:

Your time and energy are best spent working with people who share your values, intentions, and goals.

---

## 4. Synchronistic signs

The universe will tell you when you are on the right track, or off it, by opening or closing doors by clever means far beyond your understanding. The eminent Swiss psychiatrist Dr. Carl Jung coined the term *synchronicity*, referring to "a meaningful coincidence." While synchronicity may seem to show up only occasionally, it is always present and working on our behalf. It is just occasionally that we notice it. If you raise your antenna, you can become more aware of meaningful coincidences. When you notice them and follow their lead, they will become more obvious and frequent.

I was studying with a mentor who conducted coaching sessions only in person at his home in Los Angeles. When I received an invitation to speak at a conference in San Francisco, I booked my flights in and out of the Bay Area. Then it occurred to me that this might be a great opportunity to hop a flight to L.A. and see my mentor. Since he books sessions months in advance, I didn't know if he would see me on short notice. To my surprise, he found space for me on the requested date. Then I was concerned that I might have a hard time changing my flight and I would have to pay a higher fare plus a stiff change-of-reservation fee. When I went to my airline online account to see about changing flights, I found a notice informing me that there had been a change of time on my original flight, and if I wanted to rebook I could do so without penalty. I phoned the airline, where a super-helpful agent gave me all of my preferred flights and didn't charge me any additional fee. The entire process was easy, fluent, and guided. My session with my mentor proved to be extremely helpful.

Watch for synchronistic signs that come repetitively. You may notice a particular book while browsing an online bookseller, and then hear about it on a talk show, and then a friend mentions it casually in a conversation. If you keep hearing about something from numerous different angles, the universe may be trying to get your attention to follow up.

The Law of Matching works persistently to connect you with your good. At one time I was advertising an expensive car for sale. A fellow showed up to look at it and offered me an unacceptable price. We could not reach an agreement, so we dropped the deal. A month went by and I still hadn't sold the vehicle. Then one evening I was having dinner at a restaurant with some friends, and the fellow who had looked at the car walked in. He asked me if I had sold the car yet, and I told him that I hadn't. We revisited our negotiations and made a deal. Life has ingenious ways to join people who can help each other.

You may also experience synchronicity in the form of road-blocks or adverse circumstances. If door after door closes, you may be getting a sign that this path is not for you, and you would be better off to head in another direction. You are not hitting a dead end; you have simply come to a "T" in the road, forcing you to move elsewhere. If you are phoning someone and the call drops, then you get their voicemail, then you find out they just went on vacation, the universe may be holding up its hand to say, "Take another path." I asked an electrician about replacing some faulty circuits in my house. He sent me a bid that belonged to another homeowner. I overlooked the error and pursued his service anyway. Then his system repair was fraught with errors. He ordered the wrong equipment and had to wait for a replacement. He installed a used piece of equipment that turned out to be defective. His assistant wired a circuit backward. Then another assistant was injured in an auto accident, and the boss couldn't get his crew together. I have never seen more things go wrong with one job. What should have taken a week ended up taking months, and even then it wasn't complete. Finally, I hired someone else to finish the job. That fellow got it done in a day. Looking back, I should have taken the initial electrician's mistaken bid as a sign that, though he was a nice guy, he had a hard time focusing and was not the person for the job.

The universe knows your best interests and has your back. Signs are coming to you continually. Observe, trust, and act on them.

## 5. Dramatic events

If you don't recognize subtle guidance and make use of it, the universe will get your attention in more dramatic ways, such as through an accident, health challenge, business setback, or divorce. While it is tempting to regard yourself as a "victim of circumstances," no such condition exists. Every event fits into the design of your awakening. If a challenging event moves you to discover self-defeating patterns of thought or behavior and move in a more rewarding direction, the experience has served you well. Painful events are calls for a course correction. Many people have told me that while their diagnosis or illness was initially daunting, the experience moved them to execute a major shift that ultimately improved their life. I have heard the same comment about divorces and business failures. No event is intrinsically good or bad; it is our *interpretation* of the event and *how we use it* that determines its meaning and value in our life.

Dramatic events are time-savers in that they force you to face and heal an issue that was undermining you little by little over time. Finding out that your business manager has been ripping you off is quite disturbing, but if he has been doing it in bits and pieces over the years and would continue if unchecked, the "in-your-face" discovery is an opportunity to put a halt to a harmful situation and replace it with something better. Likewise, surprise divorces should often come as no surprise; there was likely a gap in the relationship that had gone long unaddressed. On a collective level, the 2008 financial meltdown was the result of years of unethical lending practices that resulted in a fragile bubble that had to burst. A crisis or high-contrast experience in which you are forced to take a radically different path is the equivalent of rapidly ripping a Band-Aid off your skin, hairs and all, rather than a slow, steady pull that just distributes more pain in smaller increments over time. Bless dramatic signs as gifts to accelerate your progress rather than tolerating ongoing distress that would have continued or exacerbated had the dramatic event not occurred.

It is possible to evolve to a point where you don't need drama to get your attention. You can learn and grow by way of gentler, subtler signs. Jarring contrasts are required only in the early stages of awakening. Spirit needs a hefty, blunt tool to penetrate dense armor. You can advance gracefully by listening to the whisper so you don't need the slap. This is why it is so important to train yourself to attune to inner guidance and recognize signals from the universe when they arrive.

## THE MYTH:
Dramatic events are just a negative fact of life
and we must put up with them.

## THE REALITY:
Difficult experiences always come with a valuable lesson
that can move us to make an important life upgrade.

## BE REASONABLE

Sometimes guidance calls us to defy logic and do things that seem unreasonable. At other times guidance calls us to fall back on reason and do what makes sense.

I received a proposal from a company inviting me to present a series of infomercials. Their agent told me that they had been following my work and they believed I was an excellent candidate for a profitable series. I knew some people in my field, like Tony Robbins, who had become famous and very rich via infomercials. The company sent me an elaborate pro forma indicating that if the series took off, I would reap millions of dollars. They proposed that we partner and split the cost of production and the profits. My investment would be about $80,000. I did not have $80,000 lying around, but I had access to a loan. I was intrigued by the prospect, but wary. I prayed for guidance.

The company offered to connect me with several of their previous clients as references. I followed up and spoke with three of those presenters. To my surprise, none of them had made any money on the infomercials. One broke even and the others sustained a loss. Their reports were revealing. I figured that if the company was going to supply me with references, they would at least send me to people who would recommend them. If this was the best they could do, that didn't say much for their productions. I withdrew from the project and saved myself $80,000 or some portion of it.

In this case my guidance came through logical inquiry. I tested the company's references, which proved negative. The project was emotionally exciting but the facts did not justify the investment. While your project may appeal to your vision, if it does not make the cut of logic, your guidance may be going thumbs down.

At another time I participated in a large conference that had been staged annually for over a dozen years, with significant success. This year a different couple had taken over planning. While they were setting up the program, the couple had an opportunity to rent a large, fancy office space in an exclusive location for $10,000 per month, rather than work out of their home. Some new age friends told them, "Go for it! This is a test to see if you are willing to take a leap of faith. Do this as an affirmation of abundance." Still the couple did not feel right about renting the space, especially since the conference was being funded by an individual private underwriter. They could not justify spending the sponsor's money when they could just as easily work from home, which they did.

For various reasons, that year the conference was not financially successful, and it took a significant loss. When I learned this, my mind flew back to the planners' decision not to spend money on a high-rent office. Those expenses would have cut even more deeply into the sponsor's losses. In retrospect it was a wise decision. In this case the spiritual hoopla was not justified. Common sense was.

Other ventures fly in the face of logic and they work. Elon Musk bet his multi-million-dollar life savings and massive investments from others on the innovative Tesla Motors, and he won big time. If your guidance urges you to take a big risk, you may succeed gloriously. Yet you might also be wise to take logical steps and ask each one to prove itself before going farther. *A Course in Miracles* tells us, "This course is always practical"—a maxim we can apply to business as well. Keep your head in the clouds and your feet on the ground.

---

## THE MYTH:

Spiritual guidance transcends or flies in the face of reason.

## THE REALITY:

Spiritual guidance often makes healthy use of reason.

---

## CONSULT AND CONSIDER

Business today is so complex and specialized that you most likely need to hire consultants and contractors to address specific areas of your work. One of my graduate school professors told our class, "A consultant is someone who borrows your watch to tell you what time it is." If you don't know how to tell time, the service is worthwhile. If you do know how to tell time, the investment is a waste. If the consultant helps you learn how to tell time, you are making an investment in yourself.

As an entrepreneur and homeowner, I have worked with the gamut of consultants, from shady, irresponsible, foolish, and ineffective to stellar, super competent, extraordinarily helpful, and even saintly. I have worked with people who were dedicated to service and charged minimally or not at all, and others who did a lousy job and gouged shamelessly. I have received outrageous bids for a particular job and found someone else to do an excellent job for 25 percent of the first bid. I have paid numerous contractors more than they asked because they deserved it, and I have paid others less than they asked because they didn't deserve it. Some of those relationships have turned into lifetime friendships, and others have ended in gnarly arguments. When working with a consultant of any kind, the adage "let the buyer beware" was never more appropriate.

Here are some tips on how to put your guidance into action to make the most of your projects with consultants or contractors:

### 1. Do your homework.

Before hiring, discover what the field has to offer. Websites like Google, Yelp, and Trip Advisor offer a wide range of user reviews. Never before in history has so much information about consultants and products been available. You will start to see patterns based on reviews. Reviewers are generally honest. Learn from their experience.

## 2. Ask people you trust for recommendations.

People with integrity know other people with integrity. People with the same values as you know others who share those values. The Law of Attraction works impeccably on your behalf. If you have a friend or associate you trust who thinks and lives in a way you respect, ask that person for a recommendation. Don't ask people who don't have a good track record in their own field or whose values don't match yours.

I had a legal issue for which I hired an attorney who got no result. I replaced him with another attorney who took a long time, charged more, and did even less. Finally, I asked someone in the holistic community for a recommendation. This person directed me to an outstanding attorney who completed the project quickly and easily with fair pricing. If you are seeking to work with someone of like mind, ask someone of like mind for a recommendation.

## 3. Trust your gut.

Your intuition will cue you to feel good about some consultants and not so good about others. Move with this prompting. Pursue those who rise to the top of your intuition-guided list. Give preference to people you are drawn to, even if you are not sure why. Sometimes your intuition will prove incorrect, but most of the time it will be rewarded. Even if your intuitive-guided plan doesn't work out, you will learn something that will help you in the long run. Build your intuitive muscle by using it. You have help from the inside out.

## 4. Take the consultant for a test drive.

Never make a long-term commitment to a person or company without a sample experience of working with them. On the playing field of action, people reveal their true colors. I once hired an administrative assistant partly because she had formatted a very professional and attractive resume. I was impressed by her presentation. After a few days on the job, she proved inept. In our exit discussion she admitted that someone else had created her resume for her. The positive impression I had formed was not based on her actual abilities.

If possible, give a candidate a small test project to see how they do. If you like their work, you can give them more. If not, you can turn elsewhere. Some people work their way into jobs with smoke and mirrors. They are all talk and no results. Others are the real deal. The Bible tells us, "By their fruits you shall know them." The true test of any person, product, or endeavor is the results they obtain. Pay the least attention to words and the most attention to actions. People who say the most usually do the least. People who say the least usually do the most.

I watch my dog evaluate a new food when I offer it to him. First he looks at it. If it appeals to his sight, he approaches it. Then he sniffs it. If it passes the smell test, he licks it. If he likes the lick, he chews it. If it tastes good, he swallows it. Any food has to pass four tests before it gets into his body. Even then, if it does not sit well in his stomach he throws it up. Human beings are often not as discerning. We see and swallow before smelling, licking, or tasting. We keep trying to digest things that are indigestible. Dogs also use a sixth sense when evaluating people. If someone has good energy the dog will go to that person, trust them, and play with them. If the person has bad energy, the dog will keep its distance, bark, and even threaten the person. Pets are some of the best teachers of a lifetime. If you want to learn devotion, joy, discernment, and healthy boundary setting, study with your dog. Cats also serve as good teachers through their own subtle senses.

Character reveals itself over time. Give someone time to show who they are. You may be disappointed, but you may also be pleasantly surprised. Native Americans ask of any project, "Does it grow corn?" meaning "Does something valuable come of this?" If so, plant it. If not, find what does grow corn and plant that.

> ## THE MYTH:
> You must make major commitments with insufficient information and then hope for the best.
>
> ## THE REALITY:
> You can take initial steps without a major commitment and then decide if you wish to continue.

## 5. Use every experience to advance your business and personal growth.

Every interaction has value. Even if a business or personal relationship doesn't work out as you expected, there is a reason for it. Find the reason, and all experiences will become your friends.

When Dee and I were planning to build a house on a rural property we purchased, we invited an architect to visit the site as a prelude to possibly hiring him. We showed him our building site on a plateau beside a hill. Then he looked up to the top of a hill and suggested we build there. We hadn't thought about that spot, but when he told us its advantages, we realized that his idea was better than ours.

When the architect submitted his bid, we realized his style did not match our taste and he was out of our price range. He was more of a commercial designer. So we did not hire him. But we did gain something from meeting with him. He said he enjoyed walking the property in nature and getting to know us. We later recommended him to some potential clients who matched his niche.

Every encounter brings some kind of gift. Sometimes the gift is the one expected, and sometimes it delivers a different kind of benefit. The shortsighted ego sees wastes of time, but the far-seeing Spirit recognizes purpose. Getting what we don't want helps us clarify what we do want and motivates us to move in that direction. Value is always present if we are open to seeing through appreciative eyes.

## TURN A MINUS INTO A PLUS

While a friend of mine was going through a rough period in his life, he suggested I write a book called *Why Your Life Sucks.* Shortly afterward a publisher asked me to write a book for her company. When she probed to see if I had some ideas on a subject, I offered several themes and jokingly told her a friend had suggested I write *Why Your Life Sucks.* Hearing that, she lit up. "That's the book I want!" she spouted.

Hearing that, my life began to suck. I had not taken the topic seriously; it was more of a joke. Now she wanted me to write a book with an in-your-face title. I balked, but she insisted. She offered me a large advance and promised a big promotional campaign.

*Now what do I do?*

After wrestling with the project for a while, I decided to make it an exciting challenge. Even though the title sounded rather negative, I could imbue the book with positive, inspiring ideas and practices. Maybe the catchy title would get people's attention, and when they got into the text I could take them to an uplifting place. I could also inject humor to lighten the journey. My energy shifted, and I began to feel creative and motivated to write.

*Why Your Life Sucks and What You Can Do About It* was met with a very positive reception. I was interviewed at the breaking news desk live on CNN. The public relations company commissioned Gallup to do a national poll asking many people, "Why does your life suck?" I gave a copy of the book to Esther Hicks of Abraham-Hicks, and Abraham began to quote and recommend the book in large public lectures—the kind of promotion money can't buy. As a result, the book has become one of the best sellers of my career. I receive thankful letters and emails from people in their teens and twenties, a population usually not in my demographic. They tell me they can relate to the title and the stories. I also hear inspiring reports from prisoners. What started out to be something negative turned into something quite positive. Even though I didn't resonate with the original idea, I felt around for a place where I *did* resonate, and I was able to steer the ship in that direction.

You can make any situation work in your favor by assigning a positive purpose to it. Turn a minus into a plus by adding a stroke of vertical awareness. Your inner teacher will show you how to transform a deficit into an asset. *You can turn anything into anything.*

## THE MYTH:

You are stuck with a situation that doesn't work.

## THE REALITY:

By using your mind and resources creatively,
you can make any situation work in your favor.

*A Course in Miracles* tells us that the ego invented the world as a place to seek and *not* find. We look outside for what can only be found inside. Brilliant success requires self-reliance. I often quote German philosopher Wolfgang von Goethe, who said, "As soon as you trust yourself, you will know how to live." To be confident in your business, you must be confident in yourself. To be confident in yourself, go within for your answers. Refute the ancient gods' prediction, "They'll never think to look there." When you do look there, you will find everything you need to know.

*A man travels the world over in search*
*of what he needs and returns home to find it.*

— George Moore

## TRUTH #2
## THE ANSWERS YOU SEEK ARE WITHIN YOU

# ILLUSION #3:
# YOUR SUCCESS DEPENDS ON EXTERNAL CONDITIONS

During the years following the 2008 financial crash, the real estate market was virtually dead. Sales flatlined, and vast numbers of real estate agents were not renewing the licenses, instead looking elsewhere for income. Lenders were not issuing mortgages. The picture was not pretty for sellers, buyers, or realtors.

Around that time, I saw my friend Nancy, a longtime successful real estate agent. She looked quite perky considering the doldrums of her industry. When I asked her how she was doing, she replied, "Fabulous! I just sold a twenty-three-million-dollar luxury beachfront estate."

I was shocked. "And how, may I ask, did you manage that?"

"Well, I heard about the house for sale, and I knew someone who might want it. I put their hands together, and the deal happened."

How simple can it get?

Nancy is living proof that success in business is determined not by trends or external variables, but by the consciousness and intention of each individual. Statistics reflect the mind-set of the masses, which is often fear-based, emotion-driven, and constricted by small thinking. Statistics apply to groups, not individuals. If you watch the same newscasts, indulge in the same buzzkill conversations, lead the same lifestyle, and give your power away to the same superficial sources, you will be subject to the same results most people create. If, on the other hand, you maintain your thoughts, words, and actions at a higher level and you source your life on rock solid universal principles, you will achieve far superior results. Never use the norm as a baseline for what is possible. Usually the norm is more of a baseline for what is impossible.

There are always people who struggle in a booming economy and people who thrive in a depressed economy. The economy does not dictate what happens to everyone. People with clear and strong intentions dictate what happens to them. You are called to be one of them.

---

## THE MYTH:

Your external conditions must change before
you can be happy and successful.

## THE REALITY:

Your happiness and success depend on
your thoughts and intentions.

---

## YOUR ROOM IN THE MANSION

To thrive no matter what is going on around you, you can—and must—generate a "bubble reality"—an experience you create for yourself independent of the experience others choose for themselves. When I visited Russia on a citizen diplomacy mission, our tour group was taken to a small town where the residents have historically venerated the Virgin Mary. Many years ago when a deadly plague was scourging the region, the people in this town prayed to Mother Mary for protection. As a result, no one in their town was affected by the plague, even while it wreaked havoc all around them. Perhaps Mother Mary protected them, or perhaps these people's sincere faith protected them, or both. In any case, the result was the same: the residents of that village created a bubble reality that yielded them an experience far different from the reality to which the multitudes subscribed.

On the island where I live, there are many real estate agents and holistic healers, among other occupations. Some of these professionals are thriving gloriously, while others are struggling to get by. "There's just not enough work. The economy sucks," some tell me. Others report, "I have more clients than I can handle; I am booked long in advance." Yet both the thrivers and the strugglers live and work on the same island subject to precisely the same economy. For one group the economy is a bummer; for the other it is a cornucopia.

We now come to a cornerstone principle that will dramatically increase your prosperity as you grasp it: *There is no such thing as "the" economy.* Many different economies coexist simultaneously as parallel realities. Each of us lives in the one equivalent to our belief. The metaphysical master Jesus explained, "In my Father's house there are many mansions," meaning that the universe is a vast estate containing many different rooms, or domains. When you enter any room, it seems like the only reality and offers compelling evidence to prove itself. The room you occupy may be the polar opposite of the room on the other side of the wall, the inhabitants of which are having an entirely different experience. Yet each room seems like the only room when you stand in it.

In the room you occupy, you have access to other people who share your belief, and no access to people who believe otherwise. The Law of Attraction connects those of like mind and intention, and sets people with non-matching intentions at a distance. This is why it is so important to be *extremely clear* about your values and goals, and then think, talk, and live them. Let the world know what you stand for and what you wish to give and receive. Stand firmly in your chosen reality, and all the right people, encounters, events, and results will recognize your intention and show up at your door, with the least effort on your part.

You don't need to wait for the economy to come around, or to sweat to make it change. You simply need to live in the economy you prefer as if it is already so, and it will demonstrate itself to be so.

---

## THE MYTH:
You are prospered or plagued by the economy.

## THE REALITY:
You choose the economy you live in and reap its results.

---

## UNIQUE BELIEFS, UNIQUE RESULTS

Nick Vujicic was born without arms or legs, a condition most people would find extremely daunting. Yet Nick has not allowed his physical condition to defeat him; instead, he has chosen to live in a state of well-being. He created a phenomenally successful career as a motivational speaker, married a lovely woman, has a family, and has established an extraordinarily happy life. So the number of limbs you have does not determine your experience, nor does your bank account, volume of clients, or the news you read. Only the thoughts and feelings you focus on determine your experience.

Elon Musk established SpaceX with the intention to build rocket ships for a fraction of the cost of the government's rockets. No private enterprise has ever challenged the model that NASA has established or their domination of the space industry. Musk was met with tremendous resistance from those who doubted his ability to pull off a win. (To discourage him, one of his friends sent Musk a 45-minute video compilation of rockets blowing up.) The SpaceX team went through three discouraging experimental launch failures, and Musk finally invested all of his remaining resources in one last launch, which succeeded. The next day NASA awarded SpaceX a $1.5-billion-dollar contract.

The nation of Costa Rica sits in the midst of countries plagued by chronic poverty, violence, corruption, and political upheaval. Yet, despite being surrounded by social and political unrest, Costa Rica is ranked number one in happiness in Central America.

The nation disbanded its standing army over 70 years ago and has devoted former military funds to education and health. Now Costa Rica leads the Latin American and Caribbean nations in health care and primary education. While the country is subject to the same influences as its neighbors, it dwells in a unique reality spawned by the values it has adopted.

Never blame people, events, or conditions for your failure, or give them credit for your success. You are responsible for the reality you live in, and no one else. Understanding this principle draws the crucial line between those who soar and those who struggle. *The world is not a cause. It is a reflection* of what is going on inside you. The world does not form your thoughts. Your thoughts form the world. Take back the power you have given to the outside world. It does not deserve it. Only *you* deserve that power. The book of Proverbs tells us, "He who is slow to anger is better than the mighty, and he who rules his spirit, better than he who captures a city." While many would-be leaders seek to rule a company, market, or nation, the real work is in ruling the mind. It is easier to boss other people than master your life. Worldly power is a cheap trinket compared to spiritual mastery. Only those who rule their own consciousness are fit to lead others because they have learned to lead themselves.

---

## THE MYTH:
You must deal with the way things are.

## THE REALITY:
You generate the way things are.

---

## GETTING PAST RESISTANCE

When setting out on an important project, you may encounter resistance. Naysayers may try to dissuade you, rules and regulations might bog you down, backers may withdraw, or other hurdles may arise. When they do, do not ascribe power to them as independent forces. Every person and event that appears in your outer world mirrors some dynamic occurring in your inner world. The master of business does not fall prey to the belief that the situations he encounters are disconnected from his own consciousness. Instead, he embraces them as representations of his own thoughts, rising to his awareness to help him transcend the limiting beliefs they outpicture. James Allen poetically stated, "We think in secret and it comes to pass. Environment is our looking glass."

Here are some specific steps you can take to move beyond resistance:

### 1. Ask, "What belief am I holding that this situation is playing out?"

You can tell what you believe by what you are getting. People or situations that challenge or disturb you are helping you see where you are harboring self-defeating undercurrents of belief, rising to the surface for recognition, evaluation, and transformation. If you get upset because someone tells you that you are not qualified for a job, is there a part of your mind that agrees with them? If funding is not forthcoming for your project, do you believe that you live in a universe of limited supply or that your endeavor may not be worthy? If your business is flatlined, what do you believe is stopping you from moving to the next level? The dots you connect between your beliefs and your results inscribe the pathway to transformation. For this reason, look firmly and courageously at your innermost thoughts projected onto the screen of the world.

My client Amy was having trouble creating the text for her website. "What page are you stuck on?" I asked her.

"It's the 'About Me' page."

"Why is that description difficult for you to write?"

"I question if I am really qualified and worth people paying me for my services."

Amy's honest answer opened the passageway to a crucial shift. "Let's hear what the voice of doubt is telling you."

"'Who are you to present yourself as a seminar leader? You are still learning from other seminar leaders. People will realize you are a phony and want their money back. Scrap your website and get a real job.'"

Amy's self-doubting voice is typical, a clear illustration of fraud guilt. That nasty demon hurls its poison arrows at just about everyone. In a moment I will show you how to defeat it. For now, let's recognize that Amy's problem was not her website. Her real challenge was self-judgment. Regarding the "About Me" page as a reflection of her mind-set was the first step for Amy to get beyond her inner critic and advance her career.

## 2. Recognize the false nature of the limiting belief you are holding.

You have been hypnotized to believe that you are less than you are and the universe is less than it is. You but dream that you are limited. You have built a dream room with dream walls and a dream ceiling and have lived in it as if it is so. You will not escape the room by pounding on the dream walls. You will escape the room by waking up. As a spiritual being, you have dominion over heaven and earth. Jesus said, "If you say to that mountain, 'Move!' it will." People connected to their Source have the power to achieve seemingly impossible results.

When faced with an obstacle, dismantle your limiting beliefs by holding them up to the light of a greater truth. Rip the costumes from the devils that make the world of fear seem so formidable. From the moment you and I arrived in the world, we were taught "truths" that contradict our inherent power. We were taught we are not good enough and we must prove ourselves; we must fight to earn our good; business is a jungle, so you must devour others before they devour you; and all manner of other twisted ideas that make no sense in the grand scheme of how life works.

My next step with Amy was to explore the origin of her critical voice so she could begin to disown it. "Who taught you to doubt yourself?" I asked her.

"My father was a newspaper editor and highly critical of me," Amy answered. "Nothing I did was good enough. If I did a project with ninety-nine percent excellence, he wouldn't compliment me on my good work. Instead, he would criticize me for the deficient one percent."

A familiar story.

"And even though you have grown up and moved out of your father's house, his voice still ricochets in your head, constantly banging at you for not being perfect."

"That's right."

I explained to Amy a key transformational principle: *The critical voice is not your own.* Every belief that burdens you came from someone who taught it to you. You were born innocent and whole, with impeccable self-confidence. You were perfectly satisfied simply being yourself. Then you were trained with all kinds of dark and demeaning programs to the contrary. As a child you were not mature enough to recognize the false nature of the illusions you were taught. You were impressionable and regarded your parents or other elders as all-knowing authorities. So you absorbed not just their critical words, but, more significantly, any demeaning energy they projected onto you. Eventually the critical voice sank into your subconscious to the point that you believed it is your own voice speaking to you. But it is not.

As an adult you can discern between the voices of criticism and empowerment and make new choices. Every business choice you make is an opportunity to honor your true self. While at the surface level you are in business to earn a livelihood, the deeper purpose of your work is to dissolve fear-based illusions and establish your work and your life in a far broader reality.

## 3. Discover the greater truth the limiting belief was hiding.

Every lie masks a truth. When you peel away myth, truth becomes obvious. Einstein declared, "Reality is an illusion, albeit a very persistent one." He also said, "When the solution is simple, God is answering." Behind the appearance of lack, there is abundant supply. Behind the appearance of vicious competition shines the redeeming strength of cooperation. Behind seeming victimhood, you are an empowered creator. Falsehood imprisons and truth liberates. If you feel depressed, discouraged, or defeated, you have fallen prey to a deception. Don't stop there. Keep going. On the other side of the wall of deception awaits the kingdom you were born to rule.

"So your challenge with your *About Me* page is just one more instance of a theme that has been going on for your entire life," I suggested to Amy.

"Exactly."

"Then let's reframe this: You are now being presented with an opportunity to finally break free from this lifelong oppressive voice that has continually challenged your progress and often undermined you."

Amy lit up. "If I could do that, it would be a turning point in my life!"

"Then let's do a role play," I offered. "I will represent your father and you can say to him what you wished you could have said when he criticized you as a child, and when his judgmental voice chides you as an adult."

Amy took a breath and sat up straight. She looked me in the eye and spoke firmly. "Dad, I know you love me and you want the best for me. But I can no longer live under the burden of your criticism. Every time I did something as a child, you found something wrong with my action and with me. Your judgments have kept me small for my entire life. I am not willing to live with them and allow them to keep impeding me."

Then came the tears.

"I am a bright woman with a good heart, valuable skills, and a significant contribution to make. I want to move forward with my new business and other paths important to me. I do not need your permission to live the life I choose and create a successful career. I now release all the dark criticisms I have borne for so long, and I step with confidence into my authentic power and a richer life."

Amy's tears cleared and her eyes shone. She looked like an entirely different person from the one who had complained about her inability to complete her web page.

"How do you feel now?" I asked her.

"Freer than I have felt in a long time."

"And how do you feel about setting up your *About Me* page?"

"Ready," she answered with a smile. "Totally ready."

A long silence ensued as Amy sat quietly stunned. Finally, she said, "It wasn't about the website, was it?"

## 4. Release others as the source of your disempowerment.

The more you blame people and conditions for your blocks or failures, the more you empower them and disempower yourself. No person or situation has the ability to hold you back. Stop making up stories about giants towering over you. *You* are a giant. But you have been programmed to believe you are a dwarf. No individual or institution is greater or stronger than you are. Worldly opinion may say so, but worldly opinion is wrong more than it is right. Take back the control you have projected onto others and you will be unstoppable.

Amy's problem was not her father, but the limiting beliefs she had learned from him. If you fight people who deliver illusions to you, you are shooting the messenger without addressing the message. People are not your enemies; illusions are. Yet illusions have no power when brought to truth. Amy later reported that she had a loving, honest conversation with her father that took both of them to a new level in their relationship.

Here is an exercise, similar to the one I guided Amy to do, that you can do to reclaim your power:

## ▪ ■ RELEASE AND ADVANCE ■ ▪ ▪

Imagine a troubling person or a symbol of an overbearing institution sitting before you. Say to that entity:

"[Name of person or institution], I have given my power away to you, and this has caused me great suffering. I have allowed you to [Describe the ways you have given your power to this individual]. I am no longer willing to make you greater or stronger than me. I refuse to allow you to control my life. I now take back the power I have attributed to you. I reclaim my identity as the source of my experience, and I choose to create success, harmony, prosperity, and well-being in my life. I release you and I release myself. And so it is."

▪ ▪ ▪

When you speak these words (or similar ones of your own choosing) sincerely, two things will happen: (1) You will feel relieved, uplifted, and strengthened; and (2) You will set in motion a chain of events that will lead to you resolving the situation troubling you.

In some cases, it may be necessary to speak these words to the person or institution they apply to. In other cases, you simply need to say and know the truth in your own mind. Remember that everyone who lives outside you represents a thought inside you. Real correction lies in your own consciousness. You can battle the world for lifetimes, but if you do not change your mind about the world, the worldly enemies persist and even magnify. Make the crucial adjustment of thought and you are free forever.

One advisory: Sometimes when you make a stand to reclaim your power, the issue you are addressing intensifies. This process is called an "extinction burst." When a dysfunctional situation is challenged, the unhealthy system recognizes that its life is being threatened, so it rears up, shows its teeth, and attempts to intimidate you to return to a weakened position. But because illusion has no substance, this threat is but smoke and mirrors. Just hang in there, hold your ground, and the dragon will yield.

## 5. Move ahead anyway.

My mentor used to say, "The dogs bark, and the caravan moves on." Even while the voices of fear, threat, and intimidation snarl, proceed anyway. Don't wait for the inner bullies to shut up before you take your next step; one of their tricks is to tell you that you can't move ahead until you have quelled them. But you can. Advance toward your goal before fear gives you permission. That permission will never come. Fear tells you that there is just one more thing to fix, one more issue to resolve, one more approval to get before you can progress. But you may have noticed that there is *always* one more hurdle to surmount. Fear festers in the illusory gap between where you stand and where you want to be. When you courageously step across that gap, you will realize that the permission you have been waiting for is your own.

### ■ ■ ■ MY FEARLESS PATH ■ ■ ■

Fill in the blank in the following statement. Repeat as many times as you can with different answers, applied first to your business world, and then to other aspects of your life. Be sure to include action steps.

*If I were not afraid, I would* _____ .

■ ■ ■

What you fill this blank with is usually your guide to the action that will advance you. "If I were not afraid, I would advertise my new business and charge the fee I choose." "If I were not afraid, I would move to a home near the ocean." "If I were not afraid, I would confront my partner about the issues of our relationship that we have swept under the rug." Fear is the insidious suffocator of passion. When you are willing to walk past that fear, you will wonder why you waited. While you may believe that you are in some way unqualified or unready, it is fear, not you, that is the liar.

Frances grew up with a demanding, belittling mother who hardly ever validated her and told her that she was unqualified at just about everything. As a result, when Frances grew up she doggedly did all she could to prove she was qualified, including obtaining numerous degrees and certificates. Eventually she developed a prestigious business with offices on several continents.

Then Frances was shocked to learn that one of her colleagues was on a vicious campaign to discredit her. He asserted that her doctoral degree was not valid and she was an impostor. Although Frances's credentials were in order, this assault threw her into a tizzy, which led her to me for coaching.

Hearing about Frances's judgmental upbringing, I was not surprised that this adverse situation had arisen. Her accuser was dramatically playing out her inner belief, "I am a phony." During coaching, Frances jokingly referred to her attacker as "Lucifer."

"Do you know the meaning of the name 'Lucifer'?" I asked Frances. She didn't. "'Lucifer comes from the same root as the word 'lucid,' which means 'clear,'" I explained. "Lucifer is the Great Clarifier. He helps you get clear on who you are and what the truth is. This fellow's attack is forcing you to look within and recognize that you are a person of integrity, your credentials are valid, and *you* are valid. If this adversary helps you accomplish this, his contribution to your life will be immeasurable."

When Frances realized that she had "hired" this man to help her heal her inner critic, she relaxed and gained confidence to deal with the onslaught. A professional conference was coming up, and although Frances had considered not going because

"Lucifer" would be there, she decided to show up and stand firmly in her worth, no matter what he said or did. When she attended, "Lucifer" did not show up, and her colleagues affirmed her validity. Frances had stepped forward to courageously face her enemy, and she emerged with dignity and grace.

At the conference Frances learned that "Lucifer" had been barred from her profession because of his own indiscretions. He was a rogue elephant on a rampage to bring others down with him. The entire episode was not about her credentials, but about her confidence in her value and abilities. "Lucifer" was an angel in disguise who helped Frances overcome a lifelong illusory limit.

One note of caution: If you are severely afraid to move ahead and the voice of fear shrieks far louder than the voice of inspiration, do what you can to shift the balance toward greater enthusiasm before you act. If you force yourself to do something you find very frightening, you may sabotage your efforts. Instead, take some time to tap into the part of you that wants to make the move, and envision how well it could work out.

---

## THE MYTH:

Challengers or attackers are your foes, come to hurt you.

## THE REALITY:

Challengers or attackers are your teachers,
come to help you advance.

---

## HIDDEN GIFTS IN CHALLENGING SITUATIONS

If you encounter difficult people or situations, here are four skills you can use to make those situations work in your favor:

## 1. Don't match dark energy.

If someone is upset or violent (even emotionally), they have fallen into a hole. They have given in to fear, ego, or illusion. If you grow upset or violent in response, you have fallen into the same hole. Now there are two people stuck. You cannot disperse darkness by bringing more darkness to it. You disperse darkness by bringing light to it. The fear-based world spins in circles going nowhere because most people react rather than act, retaliate rather than respond. Lower consciousness is combative, while higher consciousness is creative. Hold your head above your opponent's, and you will find solutions that knee-jerk reactions can never accomplish.

## 2. Learn and grow from feedback.

Even though much of what the challenging person is saying may be incorrect, there may be a shred of truth in their argument that you can make work on your behalf. Don't be quick to write off negative feedback or a contrary opinion as entirely incorrect. After I presented one of my first residential retreats, a woman sent me a letter complaining about the facility I had chosen. At first my ego bristled and I discounted the woman as a whiner. Then I reread her letter and realized that she had made at least one good point about why the facility was less than excellent. Upon second reading, I realized the lady was trying to help me. She even recommended another retreat center. When I followed up with that facility, I found it superior and used that site afterward. So what my ego interpreted as a threat turned out to be a blessing.

I used to support a political candidate who sent me regular emails. After a while I tired of his message because his party was always right about everything and the other party was always wrong about everything. I lost confidence in this candidate's message because he was so polarized. He would have been more believable if he acknowledged even a few minor merits of the other party's position. Conscious business, like conscious politics, is not based on the white-hatted good guys constantly fighting the black-hatted bad guys. It depends on seeking truth wherever it shows up, even in minor glimpses, and using it to advance your work. Even a clock that is stopped is right twice a day.

### 3. Consider that the challenging person or situation has come to you seeking healing.

While you may not agree with the difficult person, or even like them, perhaps there is some way you can help them. People who are upset are in pain. Happy, healthy people do not cause trouble. Ask yourself, "How could this person be calling for love, acknowledgment, listening, validation, compassion, or kindness?" When you reframe an attacker as wounded rather than evil, you come to see that person in a light that reveals a healing pathway for both of you.

### 4. Let this experience strengthen you.

Through facing opposition, you must dig into yourself to discover and affirm your authentic values, trust them, and stand for them. Your opponent is your master teacher, motivating you to remember the truth in the face of illusion, recognize strength behind the appearance of weakness, and choose love rather than give in to fear.

If you open the lid of a washing machine during the agitation cycle, you find gray, smelly water full of the dirt and residue removed from the clothing you are washing. If you didn't understand how the washing machine works, you would think something had gone terribly wrong; the process is supposed to clean the clothes and make them look and smell nicer, and now they appear worse. But if you know that the agitation process is part of the greater picture and the clothes will be cleaner when the muck is washed away in the next cycle, you can relax and know that everything is working as it should. Likewise, when people or events show up that agitate you, reframe the situation such that the grimy stuff has been drawn to the surface solely for the purpose of purging what has been undermining you, and the entire process will ultimately improve your situation.

## SUCCESS IS AN INSIDE JOB

While the world seems quite solid and there is mass agreement that it wields power over you, it does not. Richard Bach declared, "Your body is your thoughts in a form you can see." The world is a broader body that represents your thoughts in a form you can see. When you see "the world," all you are seeing are your beliefs about it.

You don't have to waste any more time or energy trying to change the outer world by manipulating people and events to conform to your desires and expectations. To attempt to fix the world is fruitless unless you fix your thoughts about it first. To keep banging away at a broken world is tantamount to a man walking along the street losing change out of a hole in his pocket. To remedy the situation, he gets a second job to earn more money to put in his pocket. But it all leaks out anyway. He would do far better to simply sew the hole.

Recognizing the world as your projection does not mean you stop acting to create a better world. You may still passionately engage in projects to improve your quality of life and help others do the same. Yet you are most empowered when you act from a Source far deeper than the superficial acts the world believes are causes rather than effects. Someone aware of the creative nature of thought is infinitely more powerful than someone wildly thrashing about to battle external goblins that are simply fear projected outward. Thoreau said, "There are a thousand hacking at the branches of evil to one who is striking at the root."

Success is your natural state. When you cease to shrink in the face of self-imposed limits, you achieve your goals in wondrous ways. Contemporary philosopher Robert Brault noted, "Looking back, you realize that everything would have explained itself if you had only stopped interrupting." Anxiety is an interruption of your authentic power. Fear-induced attempts to control people and outcomes distract you from the real task at hand, the mastery of your own life. It is a rare person who is willing to accept responsibility for his or her experience. It is tempting to believe that what you see is separate from your thoughts about it; that your salvation or damnation depends on the actions of others. Only you can curse yourself and only you can redeem yourself by living from what is within you rather than depending on what is outside you. Behold the confidence the Creator has in you.

---

## TRUTH #3
## ALL THE POWER YOU NEED TO SUCCEED LIVES WITHIN YOU

---

# ILLUSION #4:
# YOUR SUPPLY IS LIMITED

As I delivered my introductory talk on my radio show, I was disappointed that no listeners were phoning in. I glanced again at the computer screen that displayed callers and their questions. *Nada.* I had carefully chosen the theme for this week's program—abundance—and here I was facing total lack. Usually at least a few callers show up at the beginning of each program. But not today. I went on with my lecture, explaining that while vast riches are available to us, we must be open to receive them. Another five minutes passed—still no callers. I had the sinking feeling that I was throwing a party and no one was attending.

After 20 minutes, the screen remained blank and I felt even more discouraged. By this time in the show I *always* had callers. So I gave up expecting people to phone. If I had to just give my lecture for the entire one-hour program, so be it. Next week I would try a more interesting topic.

At the half-hour mark we broke for a commercial and I texted the studio engineer, remarking how strange it was that no one was calling. "The switchboard is all lit up," he replied. "Didn't you see it?" *Not at all.* We did some troubleshooting and found that I had logged in to the wrong switchboard screen on my computer. A few days earlier I had prerecorded a show, which required me to log in to a screen at a different URL from the one we use for the live shows. When the live show came, I had forgotten to switch back to the regular URL. I logged on to the live show URL—which was but *one number* different from the pre-record URL. There I found a large group of listeners queued up for me to take their calls.

I had to laugh. I had just proven the theme of my program! An abundance of callers was at my door, but I was not seeing them. Changing but *one digit* on the URL took me to an entirely different place that made them available to me. When we returned from the commercial break I told the listeners what had happened, and I took all of their calls—a humbling but stunning lesson!

---

## THE MYTH:

You cannot get enough of what you need.

## THE REALITY:

All you need is given and available.
You need only be open to receive it.

---

## HOW YOU LOOK DETERMINES WHAT YOU SEE

There are two ways of looking at resources: *horizontal* and *vertical*. The horizontal view is based on limited supply. We have ten loaves of bread and ten hungry people. Everyone gets a loaf. If ten more people show up, everyone gets half a loaf. Ten more, and the portion shrinks to one-third of a loaf. The more people, the less food for each one. If one person hogs several portions of bread, others are deprived. English economist Thomas Malthus based his entire theory of economics and dire warnings of mass shortage on limited horizontal supply. Too many people for too few resources.

This model is accurate if you see with the body's eyes only and calculate strictly with your intellect, both of which function in a dimension of severe limitation. The Higher Mind, by contrast, is aware of far vaster territory. I once went to breakfast at a restaurant with a friend and her two young sons. It wasn't long before the kids got into a fight over the pancakes. The older boy took half of a pancake off his little brother's plate and the younger child flew into a fit.

My response was to reprimand the elder brother and coerce him to return the pancake. Their mom, however, had a different idea. She simply ordered more pancakes.

The horizontal mind says (of all of life), "There are just a few pancakes and we will have to figure out how to divide them." The vertical mind says, "There is a big kitchen on the other side of that wall with lots of pancakes, so everyone can have as many as they like."

"But wait!" the horizontal mind argues. "There are a fixed number of resources on the planet Earth. There is just so much oil to power our engines. Soon we will run out, and there will not be enough for everyone."

Yes, there is a fixed amount of oil. One day we will surely run out. But there is an infinite amount of sunlight. We could supply the entire world's electrical needs using sunlight, wind, and water power, of which there is an endless supply. We could power the entire world's electrical needs with a solar array the size of a small state like West Virginia. Oil is horizontal and sunlight is vertical. Are we looking down or up?

Energy is available to us in even vaster quantities than sunlight and other physical commodities can provide. Nikola Tesla, who brought the world alternating current (AC) electricity, wireless technology, the radio, X-rays, fluorescent light, and many other boons to humanity, was in the process of developing a system by which electricity could be extracted in unlimited quantities from the earth's atmosphere. Bankrolled by mega-wealthy financier J. P. Morgan, Tesla constructed the huge Wardenclyffe Tower in Shoreham on Long Island, intended to draw electricity from the ionosphere, as a prototype for a system that would enable everyone in the world to have all the electricity they need for free. But when Morgan realized that such a system could not be metered, and electric companies could not make money on such a grid, he pulled the plug on the project. It is just a matter of time until another Tesla comes along and resurrects the project. There are already a number of zero-point energy devices available that serve as models for a universal energy supply system.

What you see depends on the kind of vision you use to see it. The limited mind sees a limited world. The unlimited mind sees infinite resources. Each mind finds evidence for its belief and reinforces the domain that matches it. *A Course in Miracles* tells us, "Faith will bring its witnesses to show that what it rested on is really there." Faith applies to anything you believe in. What you have faith in proves itself. Everyone has faith in something. Take care where you place your faith.

---

## THE MYTH:
We live in a universe of fixed resources.
We must struggle and compete to get our share.

## THE REALITY:
We live in a universe of infinite resources,
capable to provide for everyone.

---

*The Law of Supply and Demand:*
*If you knew there was infinite supply,*
*you would not need to demand.*

---

## OCCUPY WEALTH

Millions of people around the globe participated in the groundswell "Occupy" movement. Angry, frustrated, disenfranchised workers protested the huge inequity in the distribution of wealth in our economy. Demonstrators cited that 1 percent of the U.S. population owns 34 percent of the wealth, and 10 percent of the population owns 73 percent of the wealth, while the rest of us are consigned to far more meager resources, often struggling to get by.

While I would love to see economic equality become the norm, there are two flaws in the occupiers' argument: (1) Some people have the power to take away other people's good; and (2) People are incapable of generating wealth for themselves. While these beliefs are accepted by many, they actually undermine our power to gain and sustain wealth. When we reverse these beliefs, we open the door for *all* to prosper.

To truly master prosperity, we must plumb to the causational level of our lives. Let us now probe deeper into the crucial dynamic of *the right of consciousness*, the true source of the wealth we attract or repel. Each of us generates our experience by the thoughts we think, the feelings we indulge, the words we speak, and the actions we take. We are the creators of our own prosperity or lack of it. Our lives are the result of the choices we make, not what others choose for us. No one else can do to you what you do not agree to be done to you, and no one has the power to take away your good.

People who dwell in a wealth mentality continually attract lots of money and hold on to it. Many millionaires have lost their fortunes, only to regain them because they know how to grow whatever money they have, starting with even a little. By contrast, someone with a poverty mentality can come into a huge fortune, but lose it because he does not have the mindset to keep money magnetized. Most lottery winners revert to their former level of wealth rather than retaining their windfall or expanding it. You probably know people who are constantly wealthy or constantly poor no matter what is given them. One of my friends is a successful businesswoman who turns any project into gold; her magic touch draws money to her like a vacuum cleaner. I know another woman who married a very wealthy man for his money and later divorced him. Although she received several homes and significant income from the divorce settlement, within several years she was penniless. She did not have the mentality to hold onto the money.

In this sense, all financial situations are fair, or at least explainable, because each of us attracts results according to our unique consciousness. This does not mean that people should settle for being mistreated or stay in an undesirable financial position because that's just their karma. Protesting for change or negotiating for more may be a part of one's path to claim greater wealth. Yet one thing is sure: no one is in their financial position by accident. Unbendable universal laws form the platform of our experience.

---

## THE MYTH:

Some people having more causes
other people to have less.

## THE REALITY:

Everyone can be wealthy without
infringing on anyone else's wealth.

---

## HOW TO INCREASE WEALTH

There is an economic theory that if all the money in the world were redistributed equally among all the people of the world, before long the money would be back in its original hands in its original proportions.

The answer to poverty is not to simply take money from the rich and give it to the poor. Or to work harder under your current mind-set. The answer is to upgrade the consciousness of the poor so they know they deserve riches and make good use of the resources within and around them. I know a New York City minister who was getting ready for the Sunday service when a woman with a baby approached him and asked for a handout because they were hungry. The minister gave her $50 to get some breakfast and groceries. The woman returned after the service and told the minister that she and her child were still hungry. "What did you do with the money I gave you this morning?" he asked. "I bought some lottery tickets," she replied.

By contrast, Starbucks's longtime CEO Howard Schultz rose dramatically from an impoverished environment. "Growing up I always felt like I was living on the other side of the tracks," Schultz recounts. "I knew the people on the other side had more resources, more money, happier families. . . . I wanted to climb over that fence and achieve something beyond what people were saying was possible." Schultz won a football scholarship to the University of Northern Michigan, and after graduation he took over Starbucks, which had 60 shops at the time. Under Schultz's guidance, Starbucks grew to more than 28,000 outlets worldwide (as of this writing), currently opening a new store in China every 15 hours. Schultz's net financial worth is estimated at $3.1 billion. Schultz is a living example of a precept my mentor taught: "Take what you have and make what you want."

I heard about a program that sought to help women in underdeveloped countries by giving them seed money to start a business. After a period of time, the program measured the progress of the recipients to see if they had grown their business. If they had, they were given more money to expand it. This was a wise way to cultivate wealth: teach and support people to use money wisely.

If everyone in the world were given more money or opportunity, a handful of people would make it work for them, but many people would not change their situation. The only thing more important than having money is knowing what to do with it. Unmotivated people wait for opportunities. Motivated people make them. Poor economic conditions influence results, but they do not determine them. Consciousness, intention, and dedicated action always supersede circumstances.

---

## THE MYTH:
You increase wealth by working harder
or manipulating the market.

## THE REALITY:
You increase wealth by upgrading your prosperity mentality.

---

## THE REAL POOR AND THE REAL RICH

Above I spoke about "the poor" as a population separate from you and me. But poverty has little to do with a bank account. Like wealth, poverty is a state of mind. Some people have a great deal of money but feel poor. Others have no money but feel rich. Wealth and poverty exist *within* us, not around us. They are not economic conditions but realms of belief. Wealth thoughts show us a wealthy world, and poverty thoughts show us a deprived world.

Redistributing financial wealth would not necessarily make people happier. Some, yes, for a while, but to others more money would be meaningless. If you have ever visited a third-world country where people are generally impoverished, you have had the stunning discovery that many people who have little or no money are far happier than many people who have lots of money. Some people with lavish financial empires are miserable, and others are soaring. A survey asked wealthy people, "Does money cause happiness, or does happiness attract money? More than two-thirds of the respondents indicated that happiness attracts money. A worldwide survey measured happiness in different nations. The happiest people in the world, according to this survey, were those in Colombia, where many people live below the poverty level. The United States, the financially wealthiest country in the world, ranked 36th among all nations in perceived happiness. So if we were to retool the Occupy and similar movements to demand equal distribution of *happiness* rather than money, we would be on the road to real riches.

The nation of Bhutan has discovered this liberating principle and put it into action. The King of Bhutan established a policy for the country: Its success is measured not by Gross Domestic Product but by Gross Domestic Happiness. As a result, the Bhutanese people are among the happiest on the planet. If we were to adopt the same standard, we could join the ranks of the wealthiest nations.

I always laugh when I read about a wealthy person's "net worth." This value is always calculated in currency. Real net worth is based on the inherent value a human being possesses simply by existing. The Creator has imbued infinite worth in every person and every living thing. That value could never be measured in money. I once went to an automotive shop for a minor repair that cost $75. I happened to have my dog Munchie in the car with me. When the repair shop owner saw the dog, he said, "I will trade you the repair for the dog." I almost fell over laughing. That dog was my best friend, my loyal companion, and the love of my life. To trade the gift of a lifetime for $75 was a joke of cosmic proportion. I told the repairman that no amount of money could equal my dog's value, and I gladly gave him the $75 instead. Jesus said, "Render unto Caesar what is due Caesar, and render unto God what is due God." Worldly things have their value and spiritual gifts have their value. There is no crossover between the two.

---

## THE MYTH:
Money is the indicator of wealth.

## THE REALITY:
Quality of life is the real indicator of wealth.

---

## WHERE MONEY COMES FROM

The notion that some people deprive others of money is unsubstantiated because there is not a fixed amount of money in the world. The amount of money in the world is always growing in proportion to the productivity of its citizens. If there is a fixed volume of money in the nation and the world, why is there more money each year? If an existing industry, such as typewriter manufacturing, produces a certain amount of money, and a new industry comes along, like computer hardware and software, that far exceeds the money generated by the old one, where does that new money come from? The answer is that wealth is generated by productivity, activity, and innovation—three commodities not fixed by an amount of money in circulation. The economy *reflects* productivity; it does not create or limit it.

Seen in this light, one person's income does not detract from another's. One person's or company's increased income actually *expands* others' opportunities to create wealth, since those who make money rarely hide it under a mattress, but instead pass it around through various purchases and investments. Every person in the world can potentially become extremely wealthy without detracting from the wealth of others. When we tap into unlimited universal prosperity principles, *everyone can be rich.*

In my town there were three natural foods stores within a ten-mile radius. Then Whole Foods Markets announced it was building a huge supermarket in the middle of the zone occupied by the other stores, within a mile of two of them. I expected that Whole Foods, with its massive inventory and slick service, would put the other stores out of business. I was completely wrong. Now, eight years after Whole Foods' entrance, all the stores are booming like never before, and two are expanding. Whole Foods actually *stimulated* interest and demand for natural foods, which spilt to the other vendors, demonstrating there is no circumference on the organic pie.

## BE RICH NOW

To increase your assets, begin by acknowledging and celebrating your current assets, whatever they may be. Feeling prosperous *now* is the first step to greater prosperity. The brilliant metaphysician Neville Goddard eloquently illuminated the Law of Reversibility. You know that if you obtained a desired goal, such as a new car, you would feel prosperous. But, according to the Law of Reversibility, if you find a way to feel prosperous *now*, you achieve two significant results: (1) You immediately gain the sense of wealth you hope to enjoy when getting the car; and (2) You increase the likelihood of attracting the car. The world has the dynamics of prosperity reversed. The car does not generate a sense of prosperity. The sense of prosperity generates the car.

> ## THE MYTH:
> You gain wealth by focusing on what you are missing and striving to fill the gap.
>
> ## THE REALITY:
> You attract greater wealth by recognizing the wealth you already have.

When people complain that the 1 percent is oppressing the 99 percent, they overlook their power to become a part of the 1 percent, which would then grow to 2 percent, then 10 percent, and ultimately even 100 percent. Ernest Holmes, author of *Science of Mind*, said, "There is room at the top for everyone." One of the reasons the Occupy movement did not sustain was that the movement focused almost entirely on complaining about what wasn't working and blaming others for their oppression. Hardly any time and talk was spent on creative solutions for constructive change. Here we come to a fundamental clue on how to shift from poverty to wealth: *Focus on what you want to achieve rather than what you want to get away from.* You get more of whatever you keep noticing. The truly wealthy are truly visionaries. They are so focused on wealthy possibilities that wealth must find its way to them.

Everyone in the world is already wealthy in that each person is using the unlimited power of their mind to generate their circumstances and experience. Someone who lives in a lack-filled world is using his mind creatively to generate the experience of lack wherever he looks. He is abundant in lack. Yet the same mind that created an abundance of lack can create an abundance of wealth. We are abundant in whatever we pay attention to. The first step to upgrading your abundance is to upgrade what you are paying attention to.

The truly wise use their minds not just to create desirable circumstances, but to create soul satisfaction. The inspiring documentary *Happy* introduces us to a half-dozen people who, by worldly standards, should not be happy at all—but they are. One of them is an Indian tuk-tuk driver who lives with his large family under a tent in a poor section of Mumbai. Meanwhile, he is one of the happiest and most positive people on the planet. He finds wealth in his family and considers his wife and children his greatest treasures. He doesn't care about getting a nice house. He already lives in the kingdom of love.

Let us each initiate world wealth by recognizing the riches within us and around us, right where we stand. Then we will occupy far more than Wall Street. We will occupy streets without any walls at all.

---

### THE MYTH:

Wealth is defined by a financial standard of living.

### THE REALITY:

Wealth is defined by a standard of thinking.

---

## WHAT PEOPLE FIND MONEY FOR

People find money for the things they value. They do not find money for things they don't value. It's as simple as that. All else is excuse, distraction, complication, and smoke and mirrors.

A woman signed up for my residential Life Mastery Training in Hawaii. She explained that she had been out of work for a while and requested a tuition discount. She seemed sincere and I agreed to a partial scholarship. When the time came for her to reserve and pay the retreat center for her room for her five-day stay, my office manager explained her choice of rooms, ranging from $795 for a triple accommodation to $1,295 for a single room. "Oh, I'll take the single!" she answered promptly. "This will be my birthday treat to myself."

Hearing this, I scratched my head and wondered why the woman could not afford the program—the tuition for which was less than the cost of a single accommodation—but, when given the opportunity to have her own room, easily found the money for it.

At another time I gave a scholarship to a fellow who had just gotten divorced and was trying to get back on his feet. After the program I phoned him to find out how he was doing. He gleefully reported that he was enjoying the new $1,000 rug he had just purchased.

I had a tenant who had a hard time paying his rent. One day he told me he would be away for a week. "Where are you going?" I asked him. "I am going to Texas to audition for *Jeopardy,*" he replied. This fellow was short a few hundred dollars for rent, but found far more funds to travel from Hawaii to Texas for a game show.

On the other side of the coin, I have seen students manifest tuition money in ingenious and even miraculous ways. One student found some saxophones in his attic and sold them. Others attract gifts from relatives, unexpected tax refunds, and lottery wins. Some get their company to sponsor them. One woman organized a fundraiser at her church. One fellow followed his intuition to attend even though the tuition plus travel costs were a stretch for him. During the seminar, another student gave him a stock market tip that he followed, and he made back all the money he had spent on the training and travel. Another woman decided to upgrade to a first-class airline seat on her way home from the retreat, an act of self-love she had never done before. When she arrived home she discovered an account she had forgotten about that funded the exact amount of the tuition and airfare, including the first-class upgrade. There are an infinite number of creative ways to manifest money when you want and need it. It's never about circumstances. It's all about choice.

## THE MYTH:
You can do only what you have enough money to finance.

## THE REALITY:
You find money for what you value.

## INCREASE YOUR WEALTH OF TIME AND ENERGY

Just as you find money for the things you value, you find the time and energy—also forms of wealth—for the activities you value. Intention mobilizes life force and ability. I used to take my dog Munchie to the beach, where he would wander off to sniff around. I would call him to return, but he didn't hear me. I thought he was getting hard of hearing, so I would go pick him up and bring him back. One day while he was at a big distance I was unwrapping the cellophane around a candy bar, which sounded like the cellophane wrapping on the treats I regularly gave him. The moment he heard the cellophane, he came dashing back! He wasn't hard of hearing at all. He was just selective about what he heard. When he heard something he wanted, he had all the energy he needed to run back.

There is no limit to the energy you find when you stay on track with the things you want to do. If you have lots of things you want to do, you will find lots of energy to do them. This is why some people are very productively busy. Other people are very busy, but they are exhausted because they are doing things they don't want to do. Your energy does not depend on how many things you are doing. It depends on *how much you value the things you are doing.* Just as desire and intention liberate money, they liberate energy.

We can apply the same lesson to time. You always have enough time to do the things you find worthwhile. When you do things you would rather not do, you feel overwhelmed, get tired and irritable, and you complete but a portion of what needs to get done. You can tell how much you want to do your current task by how much you are looking at the clock. The more you watch the time, the more you are waiting for the current undesirable task to be over. That is torment. On the other hand, when you do what you love, you don't care at all about the time. You are swimming in the timeless now. That is heaven.

To find more time, choose activities in which you breathe rather than suffocate. The secret to escaping the bondage of time is to immerse yourself in the now moment, the portal to eternity. When you do what you love, you establish yourself in the now. If you must do something you would rather not do, drop resistance and be playful with the task at hand. Time cannot bind you. It has no power except that which you give it. Only your thoughts can confine you. When you choose uplifting thoughts and activities, you rise beyond time and become its master.

## TAP YOUR RESOURCES

My friend Marty ran into financial difficulties and was in danger of losing his home. He fought with the mortgage company for years to keep it from repossessing his property. Every few months when I spoke to Marty he recounted the latest details of the on-going drama. He was always on the edge of foreclosure, continually soliciting funds from any source possible, narrowly escaping. At one time he appealed to me for a loan. Because he was a good friend over many years and he had helped me in various ways, I wrote him a substantial check. I knew he would not be able to pay me back, so I was happy to make the funds a gift, knowing it would help save his house.

A short time later when I spoke to Marty, he casually mentioned, "I guess I could sell my restaurant building in San Diego." I was shocked! "You have a building in San Diego?" I asked. "Yeah, it's worth quite a bit and the market is getting better, so I think I will hold onto it." I couldn't believe my ears! Marty's battle with his mortgage company took up most of his time and energy and cost him emotional and physical health. He had hit up all of his friends for loans, some several times. Meanwhile he had a hugely valuable asset that, if he sold it, could have paid off his house in a flash!

To this day I don't understand Marty's reasoning. I believe he was engaged in a totally unnecessary struggle. But we all do crazy things when it comes to money. Like Marty, we all have assets we may not be tapping. When we shift our attention from resistance to possibilities, they reveal themselves.

If you are struggling with finances, a project, or a purchase, consider if there is some available resource you have not drawn upon. You may be able to swing a loan, sell an asset, put a talent or skill into income-earning action, or find a creative way to make a deal. A friend of mine wanted to move to a bigger property and found a lovely piece of land at an attractive price. She had a home on her current property but would have to wait until she could build on the new property before she could sell the old one. A friend of hers made her a six-year personal loan at low interest, which would give her time to build a home and then sell her current property. The old saying, "Where there is a will, there is a way," is absolutely true.

---

## THE MYTH:

Your resources are unable to provide for your needs.

## THE REALITY:

You have untapped resources you can mobilize.

---

## QUIT PLAYING SMALL

When I began my professional path, I studied with a brilliant prosperity teacher, Patricia Sun. One afternoon I went to attend one of Patricia's lectures in New York City. At the time, the going rate for a three-hour seminar was $15. When I saw that Patricia's admission price was $35, I balked. I asked the ticket taker if there was a student price. I had the money, but my resistance to a higher price overrode my willingness to pay at first request. "The price is $35 for everyone," she answered flatly. Quickly I realized I was not going to talk my way into a lesser tuition. I decided that I really wanted to attend the seminar, so I forked over the 35 bucks.

When I attended the seminar I found the content phenomenally empowering and healing; I completely forgot about the price of tuition. The program was priceless and the tuition was, in reality, a non-issue. It was a small investment for a huge return.

From that experience I learned three life-changing lessons:

- When you know what you and your product or service are worth, you can ask for your fee without apology and you don't need to bargain or compromise.

- The people who recognize the value of your offering will gladly pay, and the people who don't recognize it will go elsewhere. Those who go elsewhere don't belong to you because they do not share your agreement on what is valuable. They will be in their right place with people who match their value system and you will be in your right place with people who match yours.

- Don't play small by attempting to bargain when you can pay. When you are willing to support others for their service, you stay in the flow of prosperity and draw greater wealth unto yourself.

The last of these points is crucial, for it defines you as prosperous and generous in giving, which leads to prosperous and generous receiving. You will expect to receive in proportion to what you give. If you are stingy in giving to others, the universe will be stingy in giving to you—not because the universe is stingy, but because you are limiting your ability to receive by limiting your ability to give. Life never limits you. All limitations are self-imposed. They are also self-released. At all times you are in total mastery of your wealth.

## FROM SECOND TO BEST

To stay on the leading edge of prosperity, act on the highest expression of your excitement you can achieve, even if that is not your ultimate situation. The spiritual teacher Bashar tells of a music aficionado who wanted to install a sophisticated sound system in his car, but the system he wanted was beyond his financial means. So he purchased the second best system on the market, which met his budget. Then someone broke into his car, stole the sound system, and marred the dashboard. The fellow's insurance company gave him the money to replace the sound system and fix the dashboard. When he took the car to the repair shop, the technician told him that the dashboard could easily be repaired with a single stroke at no cost. Meanwhile the fellow had a check in hand for the audio system *and* the dashboard repair, which provided him with *exactly* the amount of money he needed to purchase the best sound system rather than the second-rate one. By staying on track with his passion to the best of his ability, the universe helped him get the best of what he wanted.

It is important to recognize that this fellow walked through this process with a sense of ease, flow, and nonresistance. If he complained that he couldn't initially get the top system or made a big hairy deal about his system getting ripped off, he may have gotten bogged in a victim mentality and limited the results that came to him. Instead, he did his best to stay in a prosperity mentality, which led to his prosperous manifestation.

> # THE MYTH:
> If you cannot get what you want, you are limited to a second-rate choice.
>
> # THE REALITY:
> Staying in a prosperity mentality and acting to the fullest on what you can do will enable you to advance to what you really want and need.

## RESOLVE MIXED INTENTIONS

I wanted to sell a property I owned next door to my house. I had it on the market for a while, but it was not moving. Around that time, I participated in a seminar in which I was asked to pair with another student and talk about something we wanted to manifest. I told my partner that I wished to sell this property, but I had a number of concerns, like getting a good price, finding a compatible neighbor, and taking care of my tax obligation on the sale.

My partner innocently asked, "Why don't you just sell it?"

This woman's simple question cut through all of my considerations. Suddenly I realized that I had been standing in my own way, and I could sell the property if I chose to. I remembered, "Obstacles are what you see when you take your eye off the goal." In that moment I became 100 percent clear that it was my choice to sell the property, and I could.

A month later some friends came to visit me. While we were driving around the island, the wife of the couple mentioned, "I had a dream of living in Hawaii on a hill overlooking the ocean." I was shocked—that was precisely the property I had for sale! I took the couple to the property, they loved it, and we made a deal on the spot. That's how easily results can manifest when you become firm on your intention.

> ## THE MYTH:
> You are not getting what you want because other people's intentions or external conditions are blocking you.
>
> ## THE REALITY:
> You are not getting what you want because your intentions are mixed, unclear, or contrary to what you say you want. When you clarify your intentions, your desired results will follow.

My client Jerry owns a thriving business with about 40 employees. During coaching he confessed that he fantasized about having a new high-end sport truck. "Then why don't you get one?" I asked him.

"I worry about what my employees will think when they see me park my expensive new truck outside our building," Jerry replied. "'There goes our rich boss who has a truck we can't afford.' I pay them well, but still I don't want them to be resentful."

Jerry was denying himself what he valued because of fear of opinion. The story illustrates how we have the power to—and often do—cancel out our desires because the beliefs we hold about why we shouldn't have what we want, or don't deserve it, are stronger than our belief that we can enjoy what our heart desires.

I worked with Jerry to reframe his vision of having his ideal truck. I suggested that his employees (whom I had previously learned love and respect Jerry as a great employer) might not envy him for his attractive vehicle, but they might be inspired to work their way up in the company, or start their own business, and advance to the point where they might eventually get their own valued vehicle or other commodity. So we recast Jerry not as an object of jealousy, but as a motivational role model. He liked this reframe, and the next time I saw him he told me that he had gotten his truck and he was enjoying it. Some of his employees told him that they were happy to see him having fun with it.

If you are having a hard time attracting money or things you value, do a bold introspection. Be extremely honest about what you want, and equally honest about any voice within you that opposes your goal or believes you do not deserve it or you cannot get it. You can always tell what you believe by what you are getting—or in this case, *not* getting. If you are not getting what you want, on some level you must perceive more value in not having it. Or your fear of getting it may outweigh your desire to get it. This can be difficult to admit, but if you can identify the belief that is canceling out what you want, you have achieved the first important step to dismantling that belief. Once you identify the belief, keep examining it and holding it up to the light. You will recognize that the negating belief is untrue or even ridiculous. Negative beliefs run us—actually *overrun* us—when we do not look at them. They can live only in the dark basement of our unexamined subconscious. When we lift such beliefs to the scrutiny of higher awareness, they dissolve. Then our true values generate our dominant energy, and they attract what we want without invisible opposition.

Now it's time for you to be really honest about the beliefs you are holding that are powering you to achieve your goals, and those that are standing in your way. The following exercise will help you get clear and move ahead.

## ▪ ▪ CLEAR ON MY INTENTION ▪ ▪

*Something I want but I am not getting:*

_____

_____

_____

*What a voice in my head says about why I don't deserve it or can't get it:*

_____

_____

*How my current situation is a reflection of my beliefs:*

_____

_____

*Why my current situation seems more attractive than getting what I want:*

_____

_____

*What I fear or resist about getting what I want:*

_____

_____

*How great could it be to get what I want:*

_____

_____

*When I step into the vision of getting what I want, and how well it could work out, this is how I feel:*

_____

_____

Practice this process until you get 100 percent clear about what you want.

■ ■ ■

On my radio show (hayhouseradio.com) I used to get five or six callers per program seeking coaching. One day as my program was concluding, I looked at the switchboard to see that the show following me was already getting 10 callers before the show began. The host of that show is a psychic who briefly answers listeners' questions about the names of their angels, the color of their aura, and what they did in their past lives, for example. I began to feel jealous that this host had so many more callers than I did, and I wished I had as many as he did.

Then I started to get more and more callers, to the point that I could not get to all of them during the show. I did not like that lots of people were waiting, and I began to rush the callers I was coaching so I could get to as many people as possible. The new situation felt burdensome. I realized that I prefer to take my time with the callers and walk them through an in-depth coaching session rather than giving them just a minute or two each. When I realized it was my true intention to have a fewer number of callers than the psychic and give them each 7 to 10 minutes for our interaction, that felt more satisfying. Since then, I get a more moderate number of callers. So my intention has always been behind my results, as your intentions are behind yours. There is no such thing as a result disconnected from your intentions. When you realize that you are always creating your results, you gain the power to create results consciously.

You are already a masterful being in that your life is an expression of your intentions, with a 100 percent correspondence between what you are choosing and what you are getting. Now you can point your mastery toward getting what you really want rather than what your limiting beliefs have generated. It's time to align your life with your true values. You are not required to put up with insufficiency of any kind, which runs contrary to your nature and destiny. All insufficiency is a lie in that it denies that each of us is the source of our own experience, and that we are choosing to focus on what is missing rather than what is present. Accept the riches already given to you, and the world is yours.

# TRUTH #4
## THERE IS NO LIMIT TO THE WEALTH YOU CAN RECEIVE

# ILLUSION #5:
# YOU MUST EARN YOUR GOOD

How much do you need to work to earn a living? Forty hours a week? Sixty? Eighty? More? How many jobs do you have? How much vacation do you deserve? Two weeks a year? Three? None? Do you work evenings, weekends, and on holidays? What do you believe you need to do before you can relax? When will you be able to retire? How much do you need to prove your worth, and to whom?

My massage therapist Penny offers a skilled and soothing treatment, and radiates positive healing energy. After receiving several massages from Penny, I noticed that she always gives a 75-minute massage when only a 60-minute session is booked and charged.

One day I asked Penny why she gives a longer session than required. She explained, "In case you don't like my work, I add some extra time to make up for any deficiency."

I was floored! Penny is one of the best massage therapists I have ever worked with. Her sessions are totally worth the price and then some. I couldn't believe she thinks her work might be lacking.

Penny's attitude is not unusual. Many of us believe that our work is not good enough because we believe that *we are not good enough*. We regard ourselves as lacking, and we must constantly hustle to prove ourselves, fill in our gaps, and earn our sustenance.

*Nothing could be further from the truth.*

As a spiritual being, you are already whole. You can dream you are broken, and then sweat to compensate for your lack. But the more you hustle to offset lack, the emptier you feel and the harder you have to work to counterbalance your perceived deficiency. The operative word here is "perceived" because your deficiency is not real. When you awaken from the illusion of insufficiency, you will recognize that you were perfect and enough all along.

The belief in having to earn in order to offset a deficit calls us to one of the major reversals we must achieve to reclaim our power to succeed. Sweating to justify your income contradicts the condition of Grace, which recognizes that you deserve providence not because of what you do, but because of what you *are*. The child of a king or a fantastically wealthy person does not have to work for sustenance, which abounds in the royal enclave. Only a deluded heir would deny her inheritance and take a distasteful job to sustain already overflowing coffers. Your task, then, is not to find ways to earn your good; it is to throw off the hypnosis that you do not deserve it.

One of my clients is a psychologist in her 60s. Doris takes impeccable care of her clients, is devoted to her family, teaches at a college, and volunteers for community service projects. She is extraordinarily generous with her time and skill, and has made a remarkable contribution over a career spanning four decades. Even with all these stellar accolades, Doris still believes she has to prove herself. She can never do enough. She wants to retire but feels guilty about letting her clients and colleagues down. I have told Doris many times, "You have built up a lifetime, and probably many lifetimes, of good karma. You have helped thousands of people directly and many more you will never know about. If anyone deserves to retire or engage in more self-nurturing activities, it's you. You could live the rest of your life enjoying yourself, without working another minute, and your life would be fully justified."

While I don't expect Doris to simply retire and crochet for the rest of her days, I wanted her to get out from under the psychic burden that she has to keep working until the end of her life to validate her existence. While I told Doris that she had already worked hard enough to deserve cruising for the rest of her life, my argument was a bit of a ploy to get her to recognize her deservingness. Her right to thrive is inherent in her identity as a creation of God, just as your worthiness is hard-wired into you.

Removing the guilt-based burden to earn your good does not mean you stop working or become a sponge and take without giving. Contributing and serving are intrinsic to personal joy and service to business and community. To the contrary, when we get out from under the whip of guilt, we gain energy, insight, and creativity, and the service we render is met with the greatest success and reward.

---

## THE MYTH:

You must do more to compensate for being less.

## THE REALITY:

You are already enough. You do not have to prove your worth. Your value is inherent in your very existence.

---

## FROM LOVE TO LACK AND BACK

You came into the world innocent, spiritually solvent, and unfettered by any sense of obligation. Your parents, acting as emissaries of God, took care of all of your needs. Then as you grew older, you were trained into a sense of owing. Parents, teachers, clergy, and elder siblings did not validate who you were, but instead shamed you for what you were not. They piled upon you a mountain of demands and pressures for you to become something else. "My child will continue the family's business." "Why can't you get good grades like your elder brother?" "Quit messing around with art projects and focus on your accounting class. You will never make any money painting." Thus you developed a misguided goal to fix yourself at the expense of being who you are. From that dysfunctional training, you set out on a long and frustrating quest to stuff yourself into tiny boxes prescribed by others. Over time you came to believe that you are trapped by a million conditions you must constantly hustle to fulfill.

Nothing is more frustrating than trying to become something you are not. In the trying is the lying. The more you attempt to fix what is not broken, the more brokenness you find to fix. You can make lots of money and brandish influence in the marketplace, but if you do not know your already-sufficiency, your soul will remain hungry and you will keep chasing a carrot at the end of a stick you cannot reach.

Consider all you have done and all you are doing to earn approval, accolades, and respect. The list is longer than you realize. Ponder the social status of your job, the amount of your income, your physical appearance, the presentation of your home, the car you drive, your wardrobe, your intellectual prowess, the certificates and diplomas you have garnered, the worldly power you wield, your number of Facebook likes, and . . . and . . . and. If you did not need to prove your worth, what would you be doing differently?

Consider also whom you are trying to prove yourself to. Many of my clients are still trying to gain acceptance from relatives who died a long time ago. Though they walk the earth no more, those relatives' voices echo in our heads like haunting ghost critics. Your struggle to prove yourself is not between you and the world. It is between you and yourself. What appears to be outside is really inside. The invisible drives the visible.

## ▪ ▪ ▪ GROWING BEYOND PROVING ▪ ▪ ▪

*How much time and energy I spend trying to prove myself:*

_____

_____

_____

*Which of my work activities are based on a feeling of obligation to earn my keep:*

_____

_____

_____

*Which activities are motivated by joy, aliveness, and creativity:*

_____

_____

_____

*How I might shift my activities to proceed more from self-expression and less from earning:*

_____

_____

_____

*How I can trust that I will be supported if I place my livelihood in a state of grace rather than debt:*

_____

_____

_____

Complete the following sentence with as many different answers as come to mind:

*If I didn't have to prove myself or earn a living, I would*

_____

_____

_____

_____

Now take some steps, even small ones, to live from your inner strength rather than a need for approval.

Earning is not a condition of life established by God. It is a system people have devised that runs contrary to creation's intention. God does not test you. The universe is too busy loving you to set up an obstacle course for you to traverse. If you love someone, you do not test them; you accept, enjoy, and support them to shine their true self. Dee and I love our dogs so much that it is our joy to provide for all of their needs. They do not need to earn their keep. They deserve to be fed, sheltered, and kept healthy not for what they do, but for what they are. Each one is perfectly lovable in his or her unique way. If you have children or pets, you do not require them to pass all kinds of tests to prove their worth. If we, in our human frailty, are capable of such unconditional love, how much more capable is God of unconditionally loving us?

*　　　*　　　*

---

# THE MYTH:
What you receive is based on what you earn.

# THE REALITY:
What you receive is based on what you are.
Because you are created in the image of God,
you deserve all the gifts of God.

---

When Senator Bernie Sanders was running for the U.S. presidential nomination in 2016, his platform included government-funded health care for all. When a reporter asked Sanders why he believes everyone deserves free health care, he replied, "Because they are human beings."

Sanders understood that wellness is our natural state, and all that we need to be well should be provided. If you were trained in a "you only deserve what you earn" mentality, the idea of inherent worth and unconditional support may sound odd to you. But if you are going to upgrade your success, you are going to have to think differently about what you deserve. Grace is our natural state. Debt of any kind is alien to our nature and purpose. Grace simply asks that we receive it and reinforce our acceptance of it by giving it.

## TRUST YOURSELF TO BE YOURSELF

While presenting a seminar, I glanced at the front row to see Tom Hanks sitting just feet away from me. I was thrilled to have one of my favorite actors join my program! Minutes later he raised his hand to speak. "My name is Steve Weber," he stated. "I'm a professional Tom Hanks impersonator." Steve explained that he had been hired by Bubba Gump Shrimp Company to sit on benches beside their restaurant entrances, wearing a white suit, impersonating Forrest Gump. He had been doing this for years and was paid well for it.

"I am tired of making a living acting like someone else," Steve confessed. "I would rather create a career as me." The man's predicament is symbolic: Many of us have established careers and reputations trying to be someone we are not. Then we wonder why we are struggling financially or emotionally. The universe rewards authenticity, not impersonation. When we deny who we are, we block the flow of abundance seeking to reach us. When we get tired of acting in someone else's movie and become the star of our own production, the universe supports us with flare. Steve later sent me a link to his new website. Now he is teaching courses like "Take Personal Responsibility and Embrace Change."

Human beings are the only creatures on the planet who try to be something other than what we are. All other living things are utterly fulfilled to express themselves exactly as they were created. Trees are happy to stand in the forest, and frogs are exhilarated in their frogness. A cat would not become a dog even if it could. The moon is not jealous of the sun; it is content to light the night rather than the day. William Blake declared, "If the sun and moon should doubt, they'd immediately go out." These natural creations don't question their role, so they continually bring grace and life to the world.

I work with many coaching clients who are brilliant and talented, but plagued by self-questioning. They shred their joy and aspirations by dissecting their visions with their intellect. Through coaching, such clients glimpse their already-magnificence, and their life sets out on a new course. They drop self-judgment and step toward infinite potential. When you remember that you were created in impeccable perfection, you will lay your gifts at the feet of the universe and it will respond by blessing you with abundance by the truckload.

---

## THE MYTH:
When you imitate others, you gain the
success they have that you envy.

## THE REALITY:
When you live authentically, you gain
the only success that truly fulfills.

---

## DARE TO BE WEIRD

Many of my coaching and seminar clients feel that they are
in some way weird. They don't fit into their job, family, religion,
culture, or world. If you feel that way, at least sometimes, I have
good news for you.

First, it's not *you* who is weird. It's *the world*. *A Course in
Miracles* tells us that the world represents the polar opposite of
reality. Commonly accepted values are inside out and upside
down. Myths seem substantial and reality becomes a dream. Our
spiritual quest calls us to sort out the real from the false and establish ourselves in our true nature. Challenging commonly held
erroneous beliefs may initially feel uncomfortable, but it is ultimately liberating. The only thing more painful than confronting an
illusion is continuing to live it.

Being a misfit is not a defect. It may be your key to success.
When I hear that a person is well adjusted, I ask, "Well adjusted
to *what?*" Learning how to find your way around a mental institution does not make you sane. Real sanity rests in authenticity.
You don't need to sell out to fit in. Your impeccable guidance is
constantly calling you away from what diminishes you and toward
what heals you. If you stick your finger in a flame, your pain recep-
tors will scream that this is not a healthy situation and you'd better
get out quickly. Sadly, many people remain in dysfunctional jobs
or relationships even though their soul is screaming, "This can't

be it!" They tell themselves, "If I leave this job my family will judge me," or "If I just keep doing what hurts me, one day it will help me," or "I will learn to love him." But there is nothing noble about living in pain; God's will for you is well-being at every level. Any other situation calls you to return to the crossroads where you chose to deny yourself, and make a new choice.

---

## THE MYTH:
Being a misfit is a defect you must correct.

## THE REALITY:
Your nonconformity is your pathway to fulfillment.

---

Never apologize for, deny, or attempt to override your feelings of being different. They are arrows pointing you to stay on track with your soul's mission. In their landmark book *The Cultural Creatives: How 50 Million People Are Changing the World*, sociologist Paul H. Ray and psychologist Sherry Ruth Anderson identify a huge population they call "cultural creatives," individuals who maintain opinions, values, and lifestyles different from the masses. Many such people have historically been shunned, excommunicated, or burned at the stake for expressing unpopular beliefs. We all retain some cellular memory of being kicked out of the herd, or we fear it. But outcasts are often the forerunners of societal advancement. Elon Musk was an introverted kid who spent most of his time reading. His peers made fun of him and called him a weirdo. Now the joke is on them as he has emerged as one of the most influential world change agents of the 21st century. Pulitzer Prize–winning historian Laurel Thatcher Ulrich declared, "Well-behaved women seldom make history." And so it is for men. Eventually the odds get even.

## THE QUIRKY SIDE OF GENIUS

Many, if not most, geniuses and transformational personalities are eccentric. If you have funny little habits or oddities, you might count yourself among a unique coterie of hugely successful and highly contributory people. For example:

- **Nikola Tesla** refused to shake hands with anyone because he feared germs. He was repulsed by jewelry, especially pearls. He remained celibate in order to channel all of his energies into his scientific inventions. He developed a special relationship with a pigeon that visited the windowsill of his Manhattan hotel room.

- **Steve Jobs** sometimes ate only two fruits such as carrots and apples for weeks at a time. He believed this regimen would enhance personal hygiene and prevent body odor (but his co-workers said it didn't work).

- **Benjamin Franklin** started each day with an air bath, standing naked in open air for 30 minutes.

- Legendary professional hockey goalie **Patrick Roy** talked to the goalposts.

- Prolific Japanese inventor **Dr. Yoshiro Nakamatsu** dives deep into a swimming pool and deprives his brain of oxygen until a half-second before death. He says this is the moment when the ideas for his inventions come.

- French author **Honoré de Balzac** consumed 50 cups of coffee per day and hardly slept while he was composing his magnum opus, *La Comédie Humaine*.

- **Albert Einstein** did not speak until he was three years old. As an adult he would stop his car, pluck a grasshopper, and eat it. He played his violin while bird-watching, to the point of tears.

- Inventor **Thomas Edison** screened prospective employees by requiring them to eat a bowl of soup in his presence.

- English author **Charles Dickens** could not stand to have a hair out of place, so he ran his comb through his hair hundreds of times a day.

- NASA's jet propulsion founder **Jack Parsons** regularly recited a hymn to the pagan god Pan during his rocketry trials.

- President **John Quincy Adams** swam nude in the Potomac River at 5 A.M. every morning, even in freezing temperatures.

- Nobel Prize Laureate physicist **Richard Feynman** developed his work on quantum electrodynamics while in a nightclub watching dancers.

Maybe you're not so weird after all. Maybe your weirdness is your greatest asset. Maybe what you thought was wrong with you is what's right with you. Just because you are out of the mainstream doesn't disqualify you from vast achievement. You are in your own stream. World change agents do not apologize for their eccentricities or try to hide them. Idiosyncrasies come with the package. So just get on with your creations and make your contribution regardless of any oddness your personality has picked up along the way. Don't wait until you are normal before you claim greatness. Normality and genius are rare bedfellows. As Walt Whitman proudly proclaimed, "Not a particle or an inch of me is vile . . . I celebrate myself."

## ▪▪▪ CELEBRATING MY GIFTS ▪▪▪

What personality quirks or habits I judge myself for, or others have judged me for:

_____

_____

How these traits might matter not at all in the grand design of my life:

_____

_____

How these traits might be positive, funny, and likable:

_____

_____

How these traits might prove to be assets to my success, and how I might capitalize on them:

_____

_____

What I would do, or do more of, if I accepted myself with my quirks or idiosyncrasies:

_____

_____

### ▪▪▪ AFFIRM: ▪▪▪

*All of my personality traits give me uniqueness and character.*
*I accept, appreciate, and celebrate all aspects of myself.*

▪ ▪ ▪

## OFF THE WALL AND ON THE MONEY

That weird business idea you've been pondering may be more profitable than you think. Lots of people have off-the-wall visions, but only those with faith build on them. Some of these ventures pay off big time. Here are some business brainstorms that have turned strangeness into cash:

- **Eternal Reefs**: Mix the ashes of a departed loved one into a cement ball that sits in the ocean and creates a living reef to replace dying ecosystems.
- **Cuddle Party**: Get together with other folks seeking closeness and have a nonsexual evening of comforting touch.
- **Throx**: Get three socks of the same kind instead of two, so when one disappears, you have two left.
- **Neuticles**: Spare your neutered dog embarrassment, and commission plastic testicular implants to make him look like one of the guys.
- **Fantasy Dating Game**: Create the date of your dreams with a partner sent by an agency, so you can act out romance without the hassles of having to get involved.
- **Rent a Mourner**: Make your departed loved one appear more popular than he or she was by hiring people to fill the funeral parlor.
- **The Anger Room**: Rent a customized room you can destroy and get the rage out of your system without social consequences.
- **The Alibi Network**: These guys will cover for you when you don't have anyone else to vouch for where you say you were.
- **Chicken Sexer**: Earn up to $60,000 a year using your intuition to tell hatcheries the sex of an unborn chick.
- **"I Do, Now I Don't" Wedding Rings**: Get most of your money back after a broken engagement or a divorce by selling the ring to someone at a decent price rather than returning it to the jeweler for a tiny portion of what you originally paid.

- **Real Estate on the Moon**: Beat the rush to buy an acre on the moon for only $18.95, complete with a map and certificate. Hats and T-shirts also available.

- **Rent a Chicken**: Pay $350 for a six-month chicken rental to see how you like the experience before you commit to an ongoing relationship.

- **The Garden of Eden**: Let it all hang out in a clothing-optional RV park.

- **Mystery Auction**: Bid on an item where you don't know what it is until you open the package.

- **Bubble Popping Keychain**: You know how therapeutic it is to pop the cells on bubble wrap. Now you can carry them on your keychain for instant stress release.

- **Flatulence Deodorizer**: Self-explanatory.

- **The Museum of Bad Art**: All the art you wish you didn't see elsewhere.

- **Square Watermelons**: Leave it to the Japanese to compact the fruit for more efficient packaging and transport.

- **Chewy Jewelry**: Let your baby chew on a necklace that's safe to ingest.

- **When You Name Upon a Star**: Register the name of a star in honor of a marriage, baby, or loved one who has passed on.

- **After-the-Rapture Pet Care Insurance**: When you are lifted to heaven, a thoughtful person who has been left behind will watch your pet. (Non-refundable if rapture doesn't come on the date predicted.)

Laugh all you want—some of these businesses are earning a million dollars a year. These ventures may sound bonkers, but they are a lot more fun than sitting in an office eight or more hours a day doing tasks that leave you cold. What's the difference between these entrepreneurs and others who have thought about ideas equally or more off-the-wall? These folks acted on them. They believed in their vision even though it sounded crazy to others. Now they are laughing all the way to the bank.

## ACT ON IT

An unusual idea I have about how I might create or advance my business:

_____

_____

What the voice of fear, doubt, or self-criticism says to me about this project:

_____

_____

What the voice of trust, confidence, and creative self-expression says in response:

_____

_____

How successful this idea could become if I put it into action:

_____

_____

The benefits I could receive from doing this project:

_____

_____

How much fun I could have:

_____

_____

An action step, even a little one, I could take to bring this idea to life:

_____

_____

## A LIFE-CHANGING EXPERIMENT

If you would like to accelerate your personal and professional progress to a quantum degree, do this experiment:

(1) For a day, weekend, week, or life, trust and act on your most exciting visions. Don't doubt or second-guess yourself. If you feel moved to phone a friend you haven't seen in a long time, do it. If someone invites you to dinner and you would rather not go, politely decline. If you have a business idea you have been delaying acting on, set it in motion. Imagine that all of your inner promptings proceed from a wise and loving source.

As you do so, several important results will accrue: (a) You will feel exhilarated, breaking free of the awful whip of self-doubt and overbearing judgment; (b) Some or most of your promptings will yield you gratifying success; (c) If any of your intuitions don't turn out as you had hoped, you will learn from them and discover that all choices bear fruit; and (d) You will be less afraid and more confident to follow your guidance in the future. If you trusted your inner voice of joy as much as you have heeded the voice of self-doubt, you would be light-years ahead of where you are. As you cultivate this new habit, you will advance at warp speed.

(2) When addressing your work, projects, and relationships, notice when you act from a need to prove yourself or earn your good, and when you act from a sense of wholeness, creativity, and confidence. After observing your motivations for a while, begin to refrain from actions based on proving and earning, and tilt your behavior toward joy and innovation. Ask yourself, "If I did not need to demonstrate my value, what would I be doing differently?" Fear not; you will not become a lazy sponger. To the contrary, when you release anxiety and lack as motivators, you liberate immense creative energy to contribute in the highest way. You come up with big ideas and find solutions and direction you would not find from a fear-based mind-set. Higher vision enables you to change the world in far more helpful ways than fruitless attempts to fill an unfillable void. You are not a black hole that needs to be filled. You are a light that needs to be shined.

## FROM ENVY TO EXCELLENCE

The people to whom we try to prove ourselves are often caught on the same hamster wheel as us. When I was in high school, I looked up to my classmate Rick Brown, the quintessential cool guy. He was the good-looking captain of the football team and president of the student council. He had a popular cheerleader girlfriend and was liked by everyone. I envied Rick because he was at the epicenter of the in-crowd, and I saw myself as a distant outsider.

Years after we graduated, I ran into Rick and we reminisced. I confessed, "I was always envious of you because you were in the in-crowd and I was way out."

Rick laughed. "Really?" he came back. "I always thought *you* were in the in-crowd and I was out."

I couldn't have been more stunned. Here was a guy who had all the accoutrements of success, all the things I wished I could be and have. Meanwhile he was envying me. How insane is that? That serendipitous meeting with Rick proved pivotal for me. I realized that no matter how cool or successful we are in the world, there is a nasty, gnarly, diminutive voice in our head that tells us there is something wrong with us for which we must compensate. Sadly, many of us spend many years or a lifetime trying to fulfill that voice's demands as if a gunslinger were shooting at our feet, commanding, "Dance, sucker!"

When I turned 40 years of physical age, I had a striking insight. I realized that if I had not become happy during my first 40 years by trying to get everyone to like me, I would probably not get happier during my next 40 years making the same attempt. So I decided to give up the burden of manipulating for approval and I adopted Popeye's mantra: "I am what I am." The moment of that decision was a turning point in my life, and it can be in yours as well—at any age.

## THE MYTH:
Striving to please everyone will gain you
the acceptance you want and need.

## THE REALITY:
Following your unique path will gain you all
the soul fulfillment you want and need.

## THE REAL REASON TO DO YOUR BEST

Does releasing the struggle to earn or prove yourself mean that you blow off work, manufacture an inferior product, and take shoddy care of your customers? Not at all. To the contrary, you should offer the best product or service you can. *Why* you offer the best product or service makes all the difference in the results you reap. If you work as a salesperson to offset your fear of becoming homeless, your workday will be drudgery. If, on the other hand, you sell because the process is creative and enlivening for you, and you take delight in knowing that your customers' lives are enhanced by the product you provide, your experience will be altogether more rewarding. Work motivated by joy is not work at all. "Choose a job you love and you will never work another day in your life."

Let us now declare the end of earning and the beginning of deserving. Like my massage therapist, you don't have to give more because you are less. Give more because you *are* more.

Life and time are precious. The day you quit proving yourself and start *being* yourself is one of the most momentous milestones in life.

# TRUTH #5
## YOU ALREADY DESERVE ALL THE GOOD YOU WANT AND NEED

# ILLUSION #6:
# THE GOAL OF WORK IS MONEY

Meryl Streep is considered by many to be the world's greatest living actress. As of this writing, she has garnered 389 Best or Supporting Actress nominations and 156 wins, including three Academy Awards and eight Golden Globes. Streep's first Oscar came in 1979 for her Best Supporting Actress role in *Kramer vs. Kramer*. During the awards ceremony she went to the ladies' room and forgetfully left the coveted gold statue on the toilet seat. The statue, to Meryl Streep, was not very important. She didn't act to get the trophy. Excellence in acting was the real gold. The trophy it led to was an afterthought.

There are seven reasons people go to work: (1) Money; (2) Passionate self-expression; (3) Rewarding relationships; (4) Service to improve others' lives; (5) Egoic achievement, competitive victory, or status; (6) Fear, guilt, obligation, rote habit, or debt to tradition; and (7) Avoidance of boredom or escape from a more unpleasant situation. We might boil this list down to two basic motivations: fear-based lack and joy-based expression.

I listed money first on the list because that is the primary motivator for most people to go to a job. If you didn't need the money, would you still go to your current job? For many, the answer would be a resounding "no." Others love their job and would do it even if they didn't get paid. People who work only for money develop a love-hate relationship with it: they love it because it helps them get the things they want, but hate it because they have to do things they don't want to do to meet their needs.

For many, money has become a god to be pursued for its own sake. They chase the almighty dollar without recognizing that they lose more in the chase than they gain in the trophy. People who work only for money are not happy. The income yields a certain reward, but as spiritual beings, our deepest need is for soul fulfillment. Only those who place creativity, connection, and spiritual satisfaction at the top of their priorities can experience the benefits of a stimulating career. I have coached countless people who are miserable in the corporate world because the culture is based largely on greed and is insensitive to workers. I have also counseled people in the corporate world who enjoy their work immensely because they perceive a higher purpose in their vocation. Earn lots of money if you like, but keep spiritual well-being at the apex of your goals. At the end of your life, you will not count your money. You will count your moments of soul reward.

*The gross national product measures everything
except that which makes life worthwhile.*

— Robert Kennedy

## PASSION IS YOUR MONEY MAGNET

There is a bridge between spirit and matter that you can cross to integrate your spiritual life with your worldly occupation. Passion, your sense of inspired aliveness, is the universe's way of guiding you to a worthwhile vocation and life. When you live and work from inspiration, two important results accrue: (1) You feel fulfilled, empowered, and soul rewarded; and (2) You attract money and other forms of sustenance.

One of the most potent ways to get finances moving is to get into the stream of passion. When I am engaged in projects I love, lots of people sign up and are happy to pay for them. If I am doing a project I am not excited about, the income stream starts to dry up. Or if I do a program that has traditionally been successful, but I have become bored with it, or I fall into a rut doing it by rote, people quit signing up. When I recognize that my passion has waned, I step back and consider, "What new program would I like to offer, or how could I vary a long-standing program in a way that would be enlivening for me and my clients?" Then I make the change, and suddenly people are banging down the door to register.

You can bless stalled finances as a sign from the universe that you have veered from your passionate path. A cash flow issue is not a problem, punishment, or embarrassment. It is a wake-up call, a stimulus to make a course correction. Be honest about where your enthusiasm lives and then do what makes you most alive. When you live true to your passion, everyone wins. Your clients get the best possible product, you abide in joy, and prosperity flows to you.

## UNCRIMP YOUR PIPELINE

"But I am passionate about my project and I am still not making money. Why is that?" you might ask. Look deeper. Do you harbor any internal blocks, such as a sense of unworthiness or self-doubt? Are there aspects of success that scare you? Are you afraid that people might judge or laugh at you, or that you might fail? Such inner negations can crimp the pipeline of prosperity for a passion-based project that would otherwise succeed. In this case your challenge is not to find more passion, but to bring to light the beliefs or fears that are clogging your pipeline, and clear them. Illusions cannot stand the light of awareness. They dissolve in the face of a higher truth. Where love meets fear, or light meets darkness, the nobler traits prevail.

Business is a prime playing field upon which we discover more about ourselves and grow spiritually. If you approach business for its own sake, you will be bored and unfulfilled. You may get an initial rush, but one day you will be up late at night with a spreadsheet, tapping your fingers at a meaningless meeting, or being browbeaten by an overbearing superior, and you will ask yourself, "Why am I doing this?" Or you may be savoring a quiet moment in nature, soaking in a warm bath, or reading an inspiring biography, when an inner voice says, "You are here for a greater purpose than you have realized." You cannot afford to live at the surface of life only. A part of you yearns to live deeper. Approach business as a venue to become more alive and bring greater life to others, and it will become your friend and reveal to you all you need to know and do to prosper.

---

## THE MYTH:

To make money, you must deny or squelch your passion.

## THE REALITY:

Passion is the avenue to the greatest prosperity.

---

## HORIZONTAL OR VERTICAL MOVEMENT?

I often work with clients who are successful in business, but have hit a wall. They have mastered the domain they know and played out their skills and talents at one level of expression. Now they feel stuck and confused about what their next step is. Don is a talented hairstylist who has established five thriving salons. He told me he was thinking about setting up a sixth shop, but could not bring himself to get going on the project. I explained to Don that a sixth salon for him would represent a horizontal move. He would just be cloning his already-achievement and not doing anything new or challenging. He had saturated his skill at opening shops and he needed a vertical move instead. As we explored what that might be, Don told me he was excited about developing an app in which clients could sign up online for treatments in his salons. The more we discussed this vision, the more he realized this was his next passionate step. He was ready to play in a bigger league. When he moved in this direction, Don danced on the leading edge of his creativity and his salons flourished even more.

If you can do something in your sleep, you are probably asleep while you are doing it. On the other side of boredom or frustration, exciting, expansive new territory beckons. Unrest pushes you to claim a higher level of expression or dive within to master deeper spiritual lessons. Everything that happens to you, including feeling stuck or facing a challenge, has the potential to advance you if you work it in your favor.

The universe will not let you hang out in dimensions you have already mastered. You are constantly being called to move onward. Monotony is an impetus to find where aliveness lives instead. There is no real safety in clinging to the known or exploiting the already-achieved. Real safety lies in inspired movement. Electricity is generated by moving water or wind. Likewise, you gain the greatest energy by continually moving your life force.

Eventually we must grow even beyond our vocation. After we have chased money, power, or worldly achievement for a length of time, we ask, "Is that all there is?" Jim Carrey said, "I think everybody should get rich and famous and do everything they ever dreamed of so they can see that it's not the answer." While you may initially feel depressed that your worldly pursuits have not yielded the fulfillment you hoped for, such disappointment is a signpost pointing you to a more substantial journey. You are being called to explore richer dimensions of life and glean rewards beyond material attainment.

There is a striking scene in the movie *Notting Hill* in which Anna, a mega-famous actress, is dating William, a British commoner. Anna attends a refreshingly down-to-earth party at William's house where his family plays the tongue-in-cheek game, "Who here is the biggest loser?" The family members vie for the mock title by recounting their failures and woes. Then, to everyone's shock, Anna offers her own sob story. She concludes by saying, "And one day not long from now, my looks will go, they will discover I can't act, and I will become some sad middle-aged woman who looks a bit like someone who was famous for a while."

People who are rewarded primarily for their looks or body are sitting on a time bomb. They have their day in the sun, but eventually their appearance or physical prowess fades and they are replaced by the next wave of hotties or athletes. Then they must figure out who they are and what their life is about independent of appearances. While such a dilemma is at first daunting, it is ultimately liberating. At that moment a life immersed in presentation yields to a life of substance—if the individual is open to discover and claim it.

The business world is even more seductive than the glamour world, since in business you can go on for a lifetime chasing glitter and die before you mine the gold of the spirit. If you have had a business crisis or setback and you begin to question the purpose of business or life before you exit stage left, count yourself as fortunate. Many people depart without escaping the illusions that bind them. Blessed are those who awaken while they can, and go on to make their business activities a source of greater aliveness rather than a ticket to hell.

## THE MYTH:

You increase success by doing more of what you have done.

## THE REALITY:

You find new and more rewarding pathways to success by staying on the cutting edge of creativity and aliveness.

## SHOW ME THE EXPERIENCE

The demand "show me the money" from the movie *Jerry Maguire* became one of the all-time most famous movie lines and cultural catchphrases. But if you think about *why* we want to be shown the money, you will understand that it is not really the money we desire, but the *experience* we believe the money will bring us.

As spiritual beings, it is experience we seek, and only experience that will satisfy us. The events that lead to the experience are stepping-stones but not substitutes for the feeling we long for. Let's say you are yearning for a sleek new sexy roadster, the ad for which promises "a passionate expression of freedom with unlimited exhilaration per mile." Now let's say you take the car for a test drive, but instead of the experience the ad promised, you feel nothing, and it is simply a neutral, dispassionate act. Upon finishing the ride, you would most likely feel disappointed and unfulfilled. Your goal was not the car itself or the act of driving it. You were seeking the *feeling* you believed the drive would bring you. Otherwise, the vehicle is worthless except as a means of transportation, which you could have purchased at a fraction of the cost. The auto dealer is not selling you a car. It is selling you passion, expression, freedom, unlimitedness, and exhilaration.

So it is with money. We seek money because we believe it will bring us a particular feeling, such as freedom, power, relief from burdens, abundance, and the sense that we can have whatever we want. What we want more than anything is soul fulfillment. If you knew you are already free, powerful, unburdened, and abundant without money, money would no longer be a vehicle to salvation. It would cease to be a source of arguments and a motivation for fearful people to manipulate, steal, and kill. Nations would not need to go to war for economic interests. Money would lose its status as a god unto itself, and it would become the convenient medium of exchange it was intended to be.

Right about now you may be thinking that I am suggesting you forget about money, don a sackcloth, join a religious order, and take a vow of poverty. Not at all. I believe you deserve all the material things that would make you happy and supply all of your needs, and I want you to have them. *How* you get to your material goals is as important as *that* you get to them. If you seek things for their own sake, you have missed a crucial step in the manifestation process. If you generate good things as a result of a shift in your consciousness, you have garnered the real prize.

When I coach people who have money struggles or feel poor, I ask them to identify all the areas of their life in which they feel abundant besides money. Clients state that they are rich in family, friends, pets, health, creativity, music, art, great ideas, nature, their spiritual path, and much more. This exercise demonstrates that money is just one slice of the abundance pie, which embraces many aspects of wealth that go far beyond your bank balance. When you realize the vast wealth you already own independent of money, two important results accrue: (1) You experience the riches you believed you were lacking, and (2) Your internal shift leads to attracting money or other forms of sustenance.

Now here's your chance to discover the riches you already own, which will lead to more:

## THE PROSPERITY PIE

Choose one aspect of business that you believe you are missing or do not have enough of.

The simplest and easiest aspect is "abundance." You can also choose "support," "passion," "opportunity," or any other element of success you value and crave more of.

In the pie shape below, fill in the areas of your life, including business and outside of business, where you experience the element you believe you are missing. Even if you have just a tiny thread of connection to that feeling, note it here.

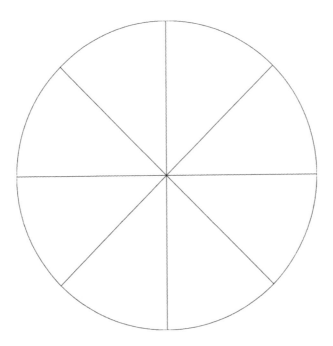

If you found even a few areas where what you thought was missing exists, and you felt even a bit more of the experience you seek, you are on your way to the critical shift that will yield you the experience and manifestation you seek.

To anchor this awareness and amplify its results, take a few minutes each day to journal your gratitude for the blessings in your life, or visualize them until you capture the feeling you desire. You will find that your prosperity pie is filled with more sweets than you thought.

■ ■ ■

Money, like all commodities, comes to you when you are an energetic match to it. You draw wealth unto you by dwelling in a prosperity mind-set. You may believe that when you get more money, you will feel prosperous, and that may be so. But more fundamentally, when you feel more prosperous you will get more money. The thoughts you think generate the feelings you feel, and the feelings you feel determine your experience. So you can create your desired experience even before its symbol shows up. Then you are truly the master of prosperity.

## THE MYTH:
You need more money to feel or be wealthy.

## THE REALITY:
The wealthier you feel, the more money you draw to you. Prosperity begins with the recognition of the riches you already own.

## FAN THE SPARK

Many coaching clients complain to me that they have no passion in their lives and they don't know what they want to do. They fear they will never connect with their joy or find their right career, partner, or life path.

Such a dilemma is more a result of limited vision than limited supply. My job as coach is to help my client unearth the passion hidden beneath fear, confusion, or a sense of deprivation. Through the coaching process, clients are able to connect with at least some passion and take steps to live it. Every human being contains a sacred spark that makes him or her want to get up in the morning and engage in a stimulating activity. In medieval times, fires were not as easy to start as they are today; you couldn't just strike a match, flick on a light switch, or turn a knob on your gas range. You had to strike flint to steel—no easy task.

To avoid having to continually start fires from scratch, people in that era carried a small steel box containing a smoldering cinder, which they sustained throughout the day by tossing in a tiny amount of kindling. Thus they could light a fire at will.

You and I carry within us a spark of spirit we can fan into a flame and energize our career and life. Your spark was created and is sustained by the Grace of God. No matter what challenges you face, how depressed you get, or what wayward paths you wander off on, your sacred ember glows. It is not yours to extinguish. It belongs to God and the part of you that *is* God. You can ignore the spark, refuse to fan it, or reduce your flame to a tiny glimmer, yet it burns without interruption. At any moment you can grow your spark into a fire by finding your passion, acting on it, and ceasing to engage in activities that dampen it. The existence of your divine spark is nonnegotiable. How much you allow it to light your life is up to you.

---

*Man's goodness is a flame that can be hidden*
*but never extinguished.*

— Nelson Mandela

---

Every business decision you make either stokes your flame or squelches it. When you set money as the sole goal of your business, you distract yourself from your inner light. Your spark may flare up when you make money, but when you take a loss it will diminish. You cannot afford to make your spark dependent on external commodities or conditions. Your flame burns from the inside out, not the outside in. The world is not the source of your spark. Spirit is. Dedicate your business to keeping your flame burning independent of events, and money will find its way to you in clever and amazing ways.

Some of my clients report that they have a passion they would like to pursue, but they need to maintain their under-stimulating but well-paying job to sustain their income and support their family.

This makes sense. I tell such clients that they do not need to engage in their passionate pursuit eight hours a day to keep their spark alive. They can play music, paint, photograph, or garden during their free time. An hour a day of immersion in joy can be spiritually sustaining. If you have a strong intention to turn a hobby into a career, you can engage in your hobby part-time for now and gradually build it into an income-producing venue. At some point you can segue from your regular job into your passionate path as your primary income producer. Many of my clients have set up creative ways to make that shift by moving their full-time income producer to a part-time gig, or rearranging their work hours to accommodate more and more of their passionate path as a revenue generator.

## THE MYTH:

You must engage in your passion as a full-time career.

## THE REALITY:

You can keep your passionate flame burning by engaging in joyful activity for at least some time daily.

Other clients tell me they feel guilty or like a sellout for taking a meaningless job rather than pursuing their passionate path. "I wish I could take acting classes and go to auditions full-time, but I need to wait tables to pay my rent." I suggest to these clients that they reframe the waitress job as being in the service of their acting career. Be grateful that your part-time job is giving you money to live on while you pursue and polish your craft. Meanwhile, make the most of your waitressing. Use your acting skills to turn on the charm to be the best waitress and maximize your tips. Develop your business skills at the restaurant. Carolyn Gable is the CEO of a huge multi-million-dollar shipping company she built herself. She wrote a book titled *Everything I Know as a CEO I Learned as a Waitress.* I know an aspiring actor who got a job waiting tables in a theme restaurant where the waiters dressed up as various movie characters. Some stars have been discovered at coffee shops. You can use any situation to further your career.

---

## THE MYTH:

If you are not engaging in your passionate career full-time, you are a sellout.

## THE REALITY:

You can use any activity in the service of advancing your passionate career.

---

Another way to lighten the burden of a relatively passionless job is to find ways to be more playful and creative within the job. Reframe your interactions with co-workers and clients as opportunities to connect, serve, and have fun. Boredom is not a given fact of any situation. It is the result of an interpretation. If you are not feeling inspired, look for ways to infuse creativity. You may not be able to change the circumstances of your work, but you can change your approach. I saw a video interview with Jeff Bezos, founder of Amazon.com, during the early days of that company. At that time Amazon was in the red by many millions of dollars, hoping to build its business into the black. As the interviewer approached Bezos's humble office, the CEO's laughter spilled down the hall. Then he laughed his way through the interview. Amazon later grew to become the most successful online store in the world, and Bezos is one of the richest men on the planet. Jeff Bezos did not wait to laugh until his company was soaring. He chose to soar right where he was, and now he is a master creator. Your life is a story you make up as you go along. You can make it a tragedy or a comedy. You can also shift a tragedy to a comedy and a triumph. Edgar Cayce said, "Mind is the builder." At every moment we are building our career and our life with thoughts we dwell on.

## BE TOTAL OR BE GONE

If passion is a money magnet, lack of passion is a money repellant. Nothing is more of a drag than working with someone who does not want to be there. When I encounter a bored, annoyed, or mentally absent sales agent, technician, or entrepreneur, I want to ask that person (and sometimes I do ask), "Why are you in this job? Why don't you do something where you could really show up and be a light to yourself and those you touch?"

We have all had the experience of checking out at a supermarket with a clerk whose mind is on anything but her job. Or the airline reservations agent who can't be bothered and finds a way to say no to every request you make. Or the accountant who is just trying to get through his day with as little human interaction as possible. It is extremely frustrating to work with someone who wishes he or she was elsewhere, who is physically present but mentally and emotionally absent.

I have worked with several business contractors who quit or retired but didn't tell their clients. One was a book designer who was a skilled and amiable fellow but no longer motivated to be in his job. Jack wanted to maintain his income but did not want to work to do it. So he acted as if he was performing his duties while he was not. Jack cut his office hours, did not answer the phone, did not return emails, and made errors in his layouts. When I actually did get through to someone in his office, I was told that Jack was fishing in the Bahamas or taking his grandkids on an RV trip through the Rockies. When I finally figured out that Jack had semi-retired without telling anyone, I switched to a designer who enjoyed his work, completed projects on time, and generated a superb product. As a result of Jack's flake-out, he developed a poor reputation and received gnarly online reviews, leading to a disappointing finale of a long and respectable career. Jack would have done better to simply announce his retirement. Or work only with the clients and projects he enjoyed. Or anything that helped him keep is spark alive. I later saw Jack after he had claimed his retirement. He looked happy and healthy when he aligned his life with his intention.

If you stay in a job you detest, you are ripping yourself off along with your colleagues, customers, and family. Your gift to the world is not so much the actions you perform as it is the energy you radiate while performing them. Your happiness draws sustenance unto you. People stay in unhappy and unhealthy situations because they do not realize that better is available to them. When you stay true to your passion, you edify your livelihood and empower those you serve.

---

## THE MYTH:

You can succeed by acting as if you are present when you are not.

## THE REALITY:

Only full presence will make you truly successful.

---

## CREATE OR DIE

The sign of a healthy plant is new growth. If that is true for such a simple life form, how much truer is it for human beings? The Bible tells us that we are made in the image and likeness of God. The Creator has imbued us with the power to create. When we are living creatively, we are most like God and most powerfully fulfilling our purpose. When we cease to create, we die physically or emotionally. A brief scan of commuters coming home on busses and trains after a work day reveals that many of us have lost touch with our power of creation; or, put another way, we have exercised our power of creation to generate a world that keeps us trapped. At any moment we can refocus that power toward liberation.

There are two ways we create: (1) Manifesting physical creations, such as works of art, inventions, products, and services; and (2) Generating a positive attitude that lifts and transforms us and the people we serve.

Category 1 creators are well known. Inventor Steve Jobs, entrepreneur Elon Musk, director Stephen Spielberg, architect Frank Lloyd Wright, and musician Bono are remarkable examples of people whose passion for a particular craft affects everyone they touch. We might also cite social change agents Susan B. Anthony and Martin Luther King, Jr., scientist Albert Einstein, and poet/writer Maya Angelou as individuals who have illuminated new paradigms for humanity and raised the bar for all. Louise Hay brought insight and inspiration to millions by revealing the connection between self-love and health. Each of these highly motivated individuals followed their voice of passion to make quantum improvements in the quality of life for their generation and all who followed.

You don't need to be an Oprah Winfrey or Walt Disney to exercise your creative impulses. Category 2 creators influence the world in subtler but no less important ways. They generate a positive experience for their customers and colleagues. Bob works in a local family-owned supermarket where Dee and I regularly shop. He is consistently upbeat, has a kind word for all of his patrons, and laughs a lot. You might say there is nothing creative about stocking shelves, working the cash register, and helping customers carry groceries to their cars. But Bob uplifts lives by establishing connection. People feel better when they walk out of the store than when they walked in. Bob will never win an Oscar and you will never see his name in a headline. But if you met him, your day would suddenly be going better. Physical creations transform the world from the outside. Attitudinal creations transform from the inside. Attitudinal transformation does not depend on circumstances. It depends on intention. If you find a way to be happy and spill your sense of well-being onto others, you are a genuine success.

## EASILY OVERCOME CREATIVE BLOCKS

Many people suffer from what they call "writer's block" or another creative impediment. They complain that their inspiration has dried up or their muse has abandoned them. Yet no weighty monolith drops between you and your creations. Instead, there are writers' (or other artists') *distractions*. Your well of creativity is always full, and you have access to infinite ideas and resources that can make you rich and happy if you tap them. If you are not drawing upon them, it is because you are focusing on something far less rewarding. You are obsessed with worry, neurotically planning, scheming to manipulate, frazzled busy, enmeshed in conflict, mired in details, straining to please others, immersed in mind-numbing screen activity, burdened with negative news, or struggling to achieve a goal you don't believe in. All such activities drag you away from your creativity, where your wellspring of success lives. You cannot simultaneously ride on two trains heading in different directions. You are going to one place or another. You cannot maintain your creativity while engaging in activities that stifle it. Stay true to your aliveness and nothing will come between you and your creations.

---

### THE MYTH:

Some condition is stopping you from creating.

### THE REALITY:

Your wellspring of creation is always
available for you to tap it.

---

If you are committed to your imaginative impulses, you can bring forth inspired expressions for the rest of this lifetime and many more. Pulitzer Prize–winning author James A. Michener declared at the age of 78, "I have at least twenty more novels I want to write before I die." I am certain that if Michener lived long enough to write them (he lived until a healthy 90, which itself is a strong statement of the life-giving power of creativity), he would find 20 more novels, and 20 more after that. When you tap into the source of creation, you step into infinity.

Here are five ways to overcome a creative block:

### 1. Engage in your creative expression even if you don't feel inspired.

Sometimes when I don't feel like writing, I just sit down anyway and start. I will look at a blank page for a minute or two, and then put something on it. Even if this piece is not my best work, it gets the ball rolling. Or I will go over a chapter in progress and see how I can fine-tune it. After a while I get into the rhythm, and the juices start to flow. I drill a pipeline into the wellspring of my creativity, and eventually it issues forth and gains momentum. Your muse has not abandoned you. He or she is tapping you on the shoulder, beaming a stream of soul-fulfilling and income-producing ideas to you. Your job is to pay attention and get into the stream.

The secret of writing is to write. The secret of dancing is to dance. The secret of managing is to manage. The secret of anything is to do it.

### 2. Do something else creative or uplifting.

If your preferred artistic expression isn't flowing, step away from that form and do something else that stimulates you. Watch a favorite movie, invite a friend to lunch, or go to a drumming party. The energy of creativity is identical to the energy of joy. When you do anything joyful, you raise your frequency, which opens the door to inspired expression in all dimensions of your life.

### 3. Quit doing what is distracting you from creating.

Above I listed a number of activities that may be pulling you away from your passion. I love the term "buzzkill," which describes any activity that depresses your creations. If you can't find your creative flow, you are engaged in thoughts or activities that are taking you elsewhere. If so, recognize that you have been seduced by meagerness or negativity, and stop whatever you are doing that is bringing you down. Exercise a "pattern interrupt" and get away from what isn't working so you can make yourself available to what will work.

## 4. Engage in a balancing activity.

At one time I lived and worked on an organic farm, which set the stage for one of the most creative phases of my life. I worked hard outside in the daytime and wrote in the evening. I deeply enjoyed the contrast and balance of being active in my body during the day and expressing mentally during the night. I would get inspiring ideas in the garden, which I set to paper when I came inside.

As a creative person, you are likely immersed in the world of intellect or emotion. You might be sitting or working in an office or studio for most of the day. You might be glued to an LCD screen or on the phone for hours. In that case you will do well to do something physical and grounding. Get into your body. Move. Sweat. Work out. Immerse yourself in nature. Get a massage. You will find that your creativity is not gone. It just needed to be balanced by the element of earth.

## 5. Put your craft aside for the moment and wait for inspiration.

All of life functions in waves, rhythms, and cycles. Timing is a key factor in any successful endeavor. If you are not feeling creative at the moment, it may not be the right time for you to express in that way. You might need to take a break and come back to your project when you feel refreshed and renewed. Perhaps you will have some experience in the interim that will enhance your project when you return to it. Don't worry—your talents have not disappeared. They are just on break. Creativity needs to breathe. There is a time for breathing in and a time for breathing out; a time for expression and a time for renewal. If you are constantly pushing yourself to create, you will end up with diminishing returns. Give yourself some space, and your creativity will find its perfect rhythm and timing.

## DARKNESS CANNOT DAMPEN YOUR LIGHT

The chief enemy of abundance-generating creativity is a sense of being stuck, confused, bored, or depressed. You might even go through a dark night of the soul. You may believe you have reached the end of your rope, and consider giving up. While such periods can be painful and frustrating, they do not need to thwart your passion or success. Moving through them and coming out on the other side will enhance your business and your life.

Here are some tips on how to navigate a stormy phase and make it work on your behalf:

### 1. Discover the course correction this experience is guiding you to make.

A challenge is never the end of the road. It is a stimulus pointing you inward and onward. How, as a result of this difficult time, might you proceed on a new path or even reinvent yourself? Some of my clients have lost their jobs due to a layoff, getting fired, business closing, or illness. I ask them, "What would you like to do that this change is giving you the opportunity to do?" Almost always, the client reveals an unspoken dream to pursue photography, healing, travel, or some activity entirely unrelated to the job they lost. Some people mobilize an entire life makeover. Looking back on the apparent loss, they realize it was an act of grace that led them to a huge gain.

I coached a fellow who had been fired from five accounting jobs. I asked him a question that was obvious to me but not to him: "Do you really want to be an accountant?" He replied, "Hell, no! I want to be an interior designer." People rarely get fired from jobs they love. They usually excel in their work, generate positive results, and please their company. Most of the people I coach who got fired didn't want to be there anyway. I congratulate them on being powerful enough to get themselves fired so they can pursue a more desirable career. If you are not thriving in your job, you probably don't want to be there. Have the guts to tell the truth about where you would rather be, take steps to move in that direction, and you will soar.

## 2. Extract the inner gift from the challenge.

A dark phase may bestow gifts that lighter phases don't yield. You might be given time to regroup, introspect, reevaluate, renew, heal, and re-vision. Being out of work can be a fertile time to reconsider what you are doing with your life and make better decisions about your work, relationships, and health. I often tell people who are out of work, "Bless this time and use it to your advantage. At some point you will be busy again and you won't have the luxury to be with yourself and make important life decisions."

Challenges often motivate individuals to express a truth they have been hesitant to tell. In relationships, for example, when someone has an affair that comes to light, or some other painful issue confronts the couple, partners start telling more truth about their feelings and experiences. Very often such honesty propels a stagnant relationship into a deeper level of communication, connection, and commitment. Other couples may part. In either case, the partners escape a rut of numbness, conflict, or loneliness. One client said of her marriage, "There is a space between us and it keeps filling up with all the things we are not saying to each other." A dark night of the soul in business can serve the same function to call forth honesty and communication that was undermining your career by not being expressed. Authentic self-expression breaks up the logjam and allows the river of life to flow again.

## 3. Use the aikido principle to create transformation.

In the martial art of *aikido*, an individual takes the energy directed at him by an attacker and redirects the power to his own advantage. Many great musicians, artists, writers, inventors, and leaders have rechanneled their grief, depression, or anger into masterful creative works and societal advancements. Composer Ludwig van Beethoven faced significant hardships, including going deaf. He composed some of his most stunning works by placing his ear against his piano and feeling the vibrations. Beethoven channeled his intense emotions into his music and created soul-stirring orchestrations that move people to tears and ecstasy even to this day. Some songwriters say they cannot compose unless they are suffering. (Let's not take this principle to an extreme and extrapolate, as some do, that suffering is required to produce works of art. It is not. Some of the greatest creations issue from moments of illumination, joy, and heightened well-being.) If hardship comes, make it work on your behalf. Write about your writer's block. Paint your sorrow. Create a seminar to help others move through the same kind of challenge you have faced. The blockbuster book and movie *Eat Pray Love* grew out of author Elizabeth Gilbert's gut-wrenching divorce. While the event was heartbreaking, it set Gilbert on a journey that led her to become a popular and wealthy international best-selling author and teacher.

### 4. Carry on anyway.

Don't let your pain keep you from creating and advancing. Even while part of you is suffering, another part is soaring. Your suffering exists in but a quadrant of your world and does not need to consume all of your experience. I wrote some of my best-selling books when I was going through difficult phases. I am glad I persevered. Metaphysically speaking, only the ego suffers. The Spirit within you remains fully intact and functional at all times. Your Higher Self is capable of generating magnificent success even while the ego experiences hardship. Don't let apparent chaos distract you from letting your inner light shine. It is there. The Spirit is not extinguishable by any conditions. It is the only part of you that is real, and the true source of your success.

---

# THE MYTH:

You are irreparably stuck, lost, or washed up.
Your work or your life is over.

# THE REALITY:

You are being pushed to the next level of aliveness, creativity, and success. The process is moving you to higher ground.

---

## WHEN SHOOTING STARS FALL

Another landmine on the road to riches is the turmoil that many famous and wealthy people experience because they don't have the character foundation to handle the intense energies and situations that accompany material success. Celebrities, entrepreneurs, politicians, the mega-rich, and people with a high public profile are subject to heavy pressure to perform, uphold an image, maintain a high degree of success, make decisions that affect lots of people, cater to special interests, and manage significant volumes of money. Famous people attract "hungry ghosts," schemers, scammers, and wannabes seeking to exploit their money, power, and influence. If the celebrity is immature or lacks a healthy value system, such pressures can be overwhelming, destructive, and even fatal. To escape pressure and overwhelm, many celebrities fall prey to addictions to alcohol, drugs, power, sex, gambling, wild spending, foolish investments, illicit deals, and other painful snares. Some stars grow sprawling, insatiable, self-destructive egos. A number sadly die young due to drug overdoses, suicide, or murder. Or they are in and out of alcohol or drug treatment programs. What started out as a dream career turns into a nightmare.

A handful of famous people are mature enough to withstand the pressures of notoriety. They maintain a healthy value system and lifestyle, and channel their influence and money into social service, charities, or activism for positive causes. Paul Newman established a hugely successful organic food company, the profits of which go to charity. Barack Obama kept his family at the core of his life and used his presidency to sincerely try to help his nation and the world. Actress Shirley MacLaine stuck to her spiritual values even though she was mocked and criticized. She said, "I can damn well believe and say what I want to. I don't care who agrees." Musician Carlos Santana is an avid student of *A Course in Miracles*. He used to connect with spiritually oriented authors Jerry Jampolsky and Diane Cirincione each morning for prayer time. One day I arrived at my office to find a huge bouquet of flowers with a note from Carlos Santana thanking me for my book *A Deep Breath of Life*, which he reads as a daily inspiration. He and others like him have established their roots in solid values, remain impervious to the pitfalls that consume so many, and use their fame and power to light the world.

One of my heroes is Dutch orchestra leader André Rieu, whose mission in life is to bring uplifting music to as many people as possible. Consistently on Billboard's list of top 10 concert earners in the world, he channels his income into ever-more creative ways to entertain the masses. While Rieu, a handsome, romantic violinist, is surrounded by attractive female musicians and millions of groupies, he remains dedicated to his family and his craft. He is one of the most beloved entertainers in the world, using his talent and position to uplift and heal.

You don't have to be on the Billboard charts to make wise use of your profession. Just bring character and integrity to whatever you are doing, and you will be a force for good.

---

### THE MYTH:

Fame, fortune, power, and influence are dreams come true.

### THE REALITY:

Fame, fortune, power, and influence can be dreams come true or nightmares, depending on what you make of them. When you keep your values in order, you will walk on solid ground.

---

Like all of the successful entertainers and world change agents mentioned above, if you hold creativity, passion, and service as your top priorities at work, you will prosper. Money is the *result* of your good work, not the *purpose* of it. We all enjoy receiving money and using it for things that make us and others happy. Soul prosperity is the real purpose for which you are here. Keep your inner flame burning brightly and all the good you seek and need will find its way to you.

---

### TRUTH #6
### THE PURPOSE OF WORK IS SOUL FULFILLMENT,
### CREATIVE EXPRESSION, AND SERVICE

---

# ILLUSION #7:

# TO SUCCEED, GET AS MUCH AS YOU CAN WHILE GIVING AS LITTLE AS YOU CAN

Motivational master Tony Robbins recalls the day he became wealthy. As a young man, Tony had loaned a friend a thousand dollars, and the fellow was not paying him back. Meanwhile Tony had whittled his assets down to just a few dollars, and he went out to buy a meal with his last wad of cash. In the restaurant he saw a little boy out to lunch with his mother. Tony was so impressed by the kindness and respect the boy showed his mom that Tony gave him all the cash he had and told him to buy his mom a nice meal. "In that moment, scarcity died," Robbins recalls. "I flew out that door. I felt so alive, so free!" The next day Tony received a check in the mail from the debtor who had been avoiding him, with interest. Robbins went on to become a mega-wealthy entrepreneur and counselor to presidents and kings. He understands that prosperity is not a bank balance. It is a state of mind. Robbins firmly declares, "You don't *get* beyond scarcity. You *start* beyond scarcity. Do more, give more, share more, and what you need will be there."

---

## THE MYTH:

The reward of wealth comes from accumulating it.

## THE REALITY:

The reward of wealth comes from circulating it.

---

## SIGNS AT THE CROSSROADS

Whether you work for a corporation, a small business, or yourself, you now stand at a crossroads in your career. The path you choose will determine the results you beget.

The signpost on one road reads:

### *How much can I get from my customers?*

The signpost on the other road reads:

### *How much can I help my customers?*

This crossroads represents the fundamental difference between the ego and the spirit, between businesses that fly and those that crash. The ego is the part of the mind that defines itself as separate, weak, and lacking. It is motivated by fear and the countless illusions that fear spawns. The ego's driving question is, "How much can I get?" and it sees everyone and everything only in terms of how it can manipulate them to fill its black hole of need. As the prevalent motivating factor in the physical world, ego-driven actions reinforce the experience of separateness and lead to suffering.

Behind the forms that carve your identity in the world, such as your body, personality, and portfolio, your true self resides as your deep inner spirit. This self sees itself and the world from an entirely different vantage point. It recognizes its wholeness and seeks not to separate, but connect. It thrives on contributing to the lives of others and finds reward in serving rather than manipulating. The Spirit recognizes that all good is shared, never in favor of one at the expense of another. Spirit-inspired actions add value to the lives of the giver *and* receiver, and melt the illusion of fragmentation.

Legendary business mentor Jim Rohn understood the importance of kindness and service in any profession. Jim's father gave him the secret of success that became the foundation of Jim's illustrious career:

### *Give your customers more than they pay for.*

Brian Johnson, founder of Optimize Enterprises, Public Benefit Corporation, raised eight million dollars building two market-leading social platform companies he later sold to publicly traded companies and parlayed his earnings to create a popular motivational institute. His motto is:

**Astonish your customers with extraordinary service.**

Put another way:

**Underpromise and overdeliver.**

At every choice point, consider how you can enhance your customers' experience and improve their lives. When you make this practice your first priority, the answers to all questions will reveal themselves and riches will find their way to your door. Whether you write code, landscape yards, treat patients, or teach students, keep reaching for the next thing you can do to put a smile on your clients' faces.

My friend Todd Hanover grew up helping his father run a furniture store in a small town. One day a lady brought a chair into the store and asked Mr. Hanover to fix it under warranty. He examined the chair and accepted it for repair. But Todd knew that the chair did not come from his father's store. After the lady left, Todd asked his dad, "Why did you take that chair for repair when she did not buy it here?"

His father smiled and answered, "She will buy her next chair here."

I went to a home supply store to buy a hot tub priced at $3,200. As I was doing the paperwork for the purchase, the customer service agent noted, "This item is going on sale next week for twenty-eight hundred dollars, so I'll give you that price." Of course I was happy to hear that. Then she said, "The product will be discontinued after that, so I will give you another five hundred dollars off." Then she found some other reason to give me a deal, and I ended up paying only about $2,000. That agent saved me a lot of money on that product. While some might argue that she was not maximizing the store's profits by giving me breaks, the contrary is true. I have become a loyal customer of the chain, and I purchase almost all of my home supplies there. In the long run the company is earning far more from me than if I had paid full price for the hot tub. That woman astonished me with service, and the company only gained.

---

## THE MYTH:

Taking a hard line on customer service
will hold the fort on profits.

## THE REALITY:

Being flexible to deliver customer service
increases long-term profits.

---

Take a moment now to consider how much your vocation is motivated by getting, how much by giving, and how you can dramatically increase your success and find peace of mind by establishing an unwavering intention to make your customers' lives better.

## ▪ ▪ ▪ THE CRUCIAL REVERSAL ▪ ▪ ▪

*Three things I seek to get from my customers:*
1. _____
2. _____
3. _____

*Three things I seek to get from my company:*
1. _____
2. _____
3. _____

*Three ways I can enhance my customers' experience and lives:*
1. _____
2. _____
3. _____

*Three ways I can help make my co-workers' jobs and lives easier:*
1. _____
2. _____
3. _____

*Three ways I can help my company succeed more:*
1. _____
2. _____
3. _____

### ▪ ▪ AFFIRM: ▪ ▪ ▪

*I take delight in contributing to my
customers, my company, and the world.
Giving others what they want is the key
to getting what I want.*

## LIFE-CHANGING DISCOVERIES

Michael Moore produced an eye-opening documentary that reveals how effectively society can work when we live in a generous mind-set. In *Where to Invade Next*, Moore visited a half-dozen foreign countries to learn how they take care of their people. He was shocked, as I was, to discover how much more compassion, service, and respect many countries show their citizens than we do in our nation. In Italy, Moore learned that workers generally receive seven weeks of paid vacation per year, plus 12 paid holidays, plus 15 days paid honeymoon upon getting married. If you don't use your 35 vacation days one year, they roll over into the next year. All of those perks are topped with an annual year-end bonus of one month's pay. Yet companies do not suffer from supporting their employees so lavishly; instead, they prosper. When Moore asked the CEO of a prestigious clothing manufacturer if the company minded bestowing employees with such benefits, he replied, "It's their right and our pleasure. The employees should enjoy the same kind of vacations that management enjoys. Vacations relieve stress, and employees return to work relaxed." At lunchtime the employees don't head for fast food joints. They go home for a relaxing two-hour lunch. Italy is among the fifteen most productive nations in the world.

In France, Moore found that public school lunches are healthy, tasty, gourmet feasts. In Slovenia, college education is free for all students. In Portugal, police officers affirm the human dignity of the population and compassionately demonstrate their desire to help people more than control them. A prison in Norway seems more like a country club than a jail. Inmates enjoy lovely private apartments with a bank of knives to cook. A rock band of guards at a maximum security penitentiary offers a welcome video for the inmates, singing "We Are the World." The documentary is astonishing, even life changing, as it reveals that the most successful countries in the world are those who seek to bless their citizens rather than exploit them.

Just as individuals prosper when they adopt generosity as their value, so do companies and nations thrive when they seek to add value to lives. Many of us are so used to charging and being charged for every little detail of our transactions that we feel confused and even stunned when we encounter a person or organization demonstrating kindness before profit. While visiting England, I had to go to a clinic for a minor medical emergency. After the doctor treated me, I went to the reception desk and asked, "Where do I pay?" The nurse looked startled. "No one pays for treatment here," she answered.

"Even if I am a foreigner visiting the country?"

She smiled. "We are happy to help you."

Then I went to the local pharmacy to pick up a couple of prescriptions. When they were filled, the clerk handed me the bag and I gave her my credit card. She waved me off: "That's all right—just take it."

I walked away in a state of stun. I am not accustomed to receiving such generosity in our medical system. Even though our magnificent nation takes care of its citizens in many important ways, including some health care, as individuals and companies many of us must pay high premiums for insurance, doctors' services, hospitalization, and medication. When I lived in Fiji, my partner was stung by a stingray and had to go to an emergency room. Again, no payment required. One of the poorest nations in the world finds a way to care for its people and even its guests. Can we do the same? How much more abundant would our nation be if we offered our citizens full health care and higher education? When we do, we will really be rich.

## THE MYTH:

Forcing citizens to take care of themselves will save a nation money.

## THE REALITY:

Taking care of its citizens will save a nation's soul.

## THE CRUCIAL SHIFT

English novelist George Eliot asked, "What are we here for if not to make each other's lives easier?" The real purpose of business is to help human beings meet their needs, get out of pain, and live more satisfying lives. Buddha called this principle "right livelihood." Everyone needs help somehow. When you make helping your first priority, all answers reveal themselves and sustenance arrives as a natural by-product.

A real estate agent told me, "The turning point in my career came when I shifted my goal from 'How can I make more money?' to 'How can I make my clients' dreams come true?' In that moment I felt a huge resurgence of energy for my career, a stream of creative ideas came to me, and since then my income has increased significantly."

Scottish theologian Ian Maclaren suggested, "Be kind, for everyone you meet is fighting a hard battle." Reframe the purpose of your work to enable people to win their inner battle. Professions or actions that frighten, threaten, or put pressure on people run contrary to right livelihood. People's lives are hard enough without someone adding to their burden. When we help lighten our fellows' load, the universe will support us. Some rewards will come through money and tangible means, and others will come through other doors. The crowning reward of a career is soul satisfaction. If you helped someone today, you will sleep well tonight. Every night before you go to sleep, take a few minutes to review your day and consider the moments when you felt genuine connection with another human being. Those were the moments that made your day worthwhile. If you are struggling with health, financial, emotional, or relationship issues, focus on being a light to others, and your personal issues will resolve. Your gift to others is your gift to yourself.

My friend Gerard was quite depressed. Then he began to look for ways to help other people to get out of their pain. He volunteered at a hospital and a few other venues. It was not long before his depression lifted. He told me, "You cannot simultaneously be helping someone and feel depressed." All healing of self or others is based on upgrading frequency. Poverty, depression, and illness all function at a dense, heavy frequency. The wavelength of service, kindness, and connection is lighter, higher, and finer. When you step into service you raise your frequency, and the causes and symptoms of poverty or illness can no longer touch you.

When seeking to rise to the next rung of authentic service and reap its rewards, don't be discouraged if you do not win the lottery on the day after you sign up to volunteer (although some people do experience miraculous providence). Set your sight on systemic enhancement more than immediate or demanded results. Attitudinal upgrade and lifestyle improvement may take a while to establish themselves and yield their rewards. Yet over time you will see the results. If you place a bowl of dirty water in the sink and let fresh water run into it, even in tiny drops, the dirty water will gradually be displaced. Likewise, wealth replaces poverty by a steady stream of wealth thoughts, feelings, and actions.

## IS IT REALLY WORTH IT?

While my friend Mark was shopping for a new widescreen television monitor, he found two local electronics stores that advertised the policy "We will not be undersold." He went to each of the stores and got them to bid against each other for the lowest price. Mark spent the entire day going back and forth between the two stores until he got a final price from one of them. "I didn't save that much," he told me, "but I got the best deal."

Hearing that, I wondered if it was really worth a day in that man's life to go back and forth in a bidding war. He was a wealthy retired attorney and could have easily afforded the first price at either of the stores. But he had been trained to bargain for the lowest price, whatever it took.

After I graduated from college, I backpacked through Europe for a summer. At an open-air market in Italy, I found a pair of jeans I liked and spent 20 minutes haggling with the vendor. When we finally arrived at a deal and I translated the cost from lira to dollars, I realized I had shaved off about 25 cents from the starting negotiation. I felt silly. How might I have otherwise spent those 20 minutes? Since that time I do my best to keep bargaining in perspective. Is the time and hassle worth it?

If you believe that you have to get as much as you can while giving as little as you can, fighting over money is worth your while. If, on the other hand, you believe that spending your time well, developing relationships, and taking care of everyone fairly is the goal of negotiation, you may not care to drag out the haggling. It's all about priorities.

---

## THE MYTH:

The person who gets the most in a deal
is the most successful.

## THE REALITY:

The person who makes the most rewarding
use of his or her time is the most successful.

---

## HOW TO GET THE MOST LIKES

Facebook offers a real-time microcosm of what works and what doesn't work in the marketplace. Followers give far more thumbs up to posts that inspire them than to sales pitches. Over all my years on Facebook, the three of my posts that received the highest number of likes and comments were (1) a video that showed a Thai policeman responding with love to a knife attacker, disarming the assailant with kindness, hugging him, giving him a drink of water, and taking him to dinner; (2) a photo of a group of Slovakian protesters who, rather than shouting and confronting police, simply stood silently in prayer and meditation; and (3) a tribute to inspirational teacher Louise Hay on the occasion of her passing. Social media readers are hungry for communication that means something to them. By contrast, my post that received the least number of likes and comments was one in which my Facebook assistant mistakenly titled the post, "Promo Video" rather than identifying the product. Consumers are tired of sales pitches, upsells, and marketers trying to get something from them. When that rare post or email arrives with a genuine offer to serve rather than solicit, recipients perk up. If you demonstrate to your customers that you sincerely seek to support them, you will win them as customers. But you cannot be kind just to get their business. Be kind because you value kindness above all else. The business will follow.

---

## THE MYTH:
The purpose of your presentations and communications is to sell your product.

## THE REALITY:
The purpose of your presentations and communications is to connect and serve.

---

Does this mean you should scrap sales and just send out touchy-feely posts of dogs licking kittens and clouds that look like angels? Not at all. When you sincerely seek to support your constituents, when it comes time for you to offer your product or service, they will trust you, pay attention to what you are offering, and be more inclined to purchase your product or service. Sandwich promotions into your communications rather than selling, selling, selling and only then offering a communication with meaning. A Facebook marketing expert told me that promotional posts should not exceed 20 percent of all posts. So it is with life. Make sales a result of connection, rather than connection a result of sales.

Likewise, take care not to use your in-person presentation as a venue for sales only. Make the sale an afterthought rather than the thought. When you have done something to improve your customers' lives, you have earned the right to market your product. I was invited to give a keynote address at a motivational conference. When I received the contract for the presentation, I read that speakers are not allowed to use more than 10 percent of their stage time to sell products. I was shocked. I would never use that much of my presentation time to market. Maybe I would take a minute or two at the end of a 90-minute program, or none at all. The organizers of that conference had obviously experienced speakers who took up a great deal of their lecture to sell their product. Such a practice lacks integrity. If a customer pays to hear a motivational lecture or other educational offering, don't compromise the program. If your listeners are impressed and inspired by your presentation, they will want to buy your product. They will recognize your sincerity and be drawn to follow up. Give your customers enough information to know what is available to them, and how they might be served by participating in what you offer. Customers with integrity are drawn to presenters with integrity. Customers who are impressed by manipulative or sleazy sales pitches deserve what they get. Ultimately they will learn that quality people sell quality products to quality customers. This is the ballpark you want to play in.

## HEART RECOGNIZES HEART

I presented a lecture at a motivational conference where I was followed by a world-famous man who had performed a celebrated heroic act. If I mentioned his name, you would surely know him and what he did; he is inscribed in the annals of history.

When I listened to this fellow's lecture, I was waiting to hear his motivational message. But it never came. Instead, he told his life story and bragged about his achievement. He failed to extract from the experience a lesson that the audience could apply to make their lives better.

After our lectures, I sat in the conference bookstore autographing my books, while the other speaker signed his books at a table next to mine. That day he was offering a special on autographs—only $85 per autograph rather than the usual $130. I have never charged for an autograph. I am happy that readers purchased by book, and I enjoy the opportunity to connect with each person and offer a brief positive message. A woman approached me in the bookstore and showed me the notebook in which she had taken notes from my lecture and the other speaker's. My page was filled with notes, and she had none for the other speaker. "I wanted to remember what you had to say because you spoke from the heart," she reported. "The other fellow was in his head the whole time. Nothing he said applied to my life."

Your product or service is valuable to your clients only if it reaches them where they live. An herbal supplement, vocational training, or home security system gives consumers the experience of health, abundance, or safety, all of which enhance their lives. Meet your customers on the ground that is most meaningful to them and you will join them in well-being.

## THE MYTH:

Talking about yourself or your product
will impress your customers.

## THE REALITY:

Talking about yourself or your product will impress
your customers only if the information is relevant to
them and they can apply it to improve their lives.

## HELP FIRST, ASK LATER

A consultant came to my office to interview for a project. As soon as he sat down, he began to rattle off his fee schedule and requirements. We hadn't even discussed the project yet. I hardly heard a word the fellow said after that, as I realized that his business was all about what he was charging. I might otherwise have been happy to pay him his fee for his services. But in that introductory meeting, I realized that his values were inverted and I didn't want to work with him.

Certainly present your fees and requirements before services commence. It's important for everyone to be clear on what they are getting into. An old country adage advises, "Make sure you shake hands before the hand is set to the plow." Establish the agreement *before* the action. Then keep the project first and payment second.

Where I live in Hawaii, business is often done more loosely than in more developed areas. Sometimes this slack backfires, since many workers don't have a business ethic and they won't show up or do a professional job. ("Couldn't make it to work today—surf was up.") On other occasions I find the relaxed attitude refreshing.

When Dee and I were planning our move from Maui to Hawaii Island, we had to find a way to transport our dogs. We did lots of research and decided to charter a small airplane to fly our furry family to a tiny airport near our new home. I found a small charter service that quoted me $1,400 for the trip. On the appointed day a pilot met us at Kahului Airport, where he helped us load our beloved "kids" onto the plane, along with all manner of possessions that filled the little craft to the brim. We enjoyed an adventurous flight across the channel, landed safely, and our dogs were excited to explore their new island and new home.

All the while the charter company had not taken my credit card information or asked any payment from me. After the flight, the pilot simply said, "Just call the office with your credit card information." Meanwhile the company didn't have my email address, my new phone number, or any way to contact me. I could have easily skipped payment if I wanted. Of course I was happy to pay them. Yet the whole experience was sweeter for the fact that the company was willing to help us and didn't make a big deal about the fee.

I am not suggesting that you just give your services away and hope that customers will pay you (although I know some people who have done this and not regretted it). In many businesses it may be wise to ask customers to pay up front. I offer this experience simply to illustrate that there may be an entirely different and more refreshing way to work with customers rather than treating them like scammers before they receive your service.

---

## THE MYTH:

People are dishonest and irresponsible and will take advantage of you if they have the opportunity.

## THE REALITY:

Most people are honest and wish to act responsibly. Your discernment will guide you as to how to protect yourself from dishonest or irresponsible customers.

---

## WHEN MONEY BECOMES LOVE

One of the best ways to overcome a lack, competition, and battleground mentality in business is to redefine money as love. Like love, money is an expression of positive energy that helps everyone who receives it. Thus all money transactions become venues to pass love around and generate more abundance. When a plumber helps you by fixing your sink, you thank the plumber by giving him love in the form of money. When you teach your class, the school loves you by way of your paycheck. If you receive a dividend from a stock market investment, the corporation is thanking you for your belief and support. While many people would say that "love makes the world go round" is an airy-fairy concept, they would agree that money makes the world go round. The two are really the same. When you reframe money transactions as venues to give and receive love, they take on a whole new meaning and experience.

Seen in this light, you can understand the utter counter-productivity of getting as much as you can while giving as little as you can. Love is more of a verb than a noun in that it works only when it moves. So it is with money. Both are valueless if you stash them away. Metaphysically speaking, you get what you give the moment you give it. Karma is not just sequential. It is simultaneous. If you give love to another person, you experience love the moment you give it. If you withhold love from another, you withhold it from yourself. So it is with money. When you are generous, you bless yourself with the experience of living in a generous universe. When you withhold money, you block receiving it because you have superimposed a sense of lack over infinite supply. Spiritual guide Ram Dass's teacher told him, "When a pickpocket sees a saint, he sees only his pockets," and "If you wear shoe leather, the whole world is covered with leather." Both metaphors teach that the world you experience depends on the vision you use to see it. When you treat money as an expression of love, you elevate your perception to recognize the presence of love moving through you and to you.

## WHAT TO DO WHEN YOU MEET THE BUDDHA

After I presented a program at a holistic health center, the director asked me if I had any recommendations for teachers for their future programs. I thought of a gifted, high-integrity teacher who would enhance the lives of the students and prosper the organization. The first question the director asked me was, "How big is his mailing list?"

I was disappointed to hear that question as the first one. The director did not ask me what this person taught, or if he was qualified, or if he was attuned to the principles of the organization. The director cared most about how many people the teacher could draw. While marketability is a significant factor in developing a successful organization, an organizer with his priorities in order would not ask this as the first question. In this case, the director had lost sight of what is most important when hiring a teacher.

There is a Buddhist saying, "When you meet the Buddha on the road, kill him," meaning that Buddha, like Christ, is a presence that extends far beyond any one body. If you are fixated on a body or personality as the source of your well-being, rather than the spirit, you must get rid of that belief. Humorous inspirational musician Scott Grace came up with a new version of the maxim: "When you meet the Buddha on the road, kill him—but first get his mailing list."

Mailing lists are vital elements of business; growing them generates valuable revenue. But when the mailing list becomes more important than the service it enables you to deliver, it has become a god unto itself, and your business is no longer spirit-based. Companies that keep integrity, service, and life force as their primary goals thrive financially and spiritually. Their mailing lists grow because people want the product or service the mailing list announces. Your best marketing tool is a high-quality product or service. All else exists to support the goal of adding value to your clients' lives.

## MONEY AS A WEAPON OF PUNISHMENT

Money, like all tangible things, is neutral. Its value and effects are determined by how we use it. For all the hoo-ha about money as the symbol of success or the root of all evil, it is but a blank screen onto which we project our beliefs about it and our intentions for it.

Just as we can use money as a venue to give and receive love, we can use it as a weapon of punishment. I hired a landscaping contractor to build a water feature in my backyard. We collaborated to design a pond with a charming little waterfall. The contractor was an amiable, easygoing chap who enjoyed co-creating this artistic project.

During the installation I made some design changes that caused the contractor a little extra work. He liked the changes and flowed with them affably, assuring me that he would stick to his original bid we had agreed on. Then I asked him if he would make the pond slightly deeper at its center. The contractor said he didn't think it was necessary, but if I really wanted him to do it, he would. I thought about it and asked him to go ahead.

When the contractor submitted his final invoice, I noticed that he had charged me extra for the deepening. I didn't mind paying him, but I found it fascinating that he had done a number of other design changes that were just as much work as the deepening, but he had not charged me for them, because he liked those ideas. When he performed a task that he did not want to do, he considered that billable.

Here we see an example of money being used as an instrument of punishment. It was clear the contractor was not charging me for his actual work on the deepening, since he had done other work he did not charge me for. He was charging me because I asked him to do something he did not agree with. Thus dollars became soldiers of guilt.

We see this principle played out in our court system, where people are sometimes required to pay money for the emotional pain they supposedly caused others. This formula reinforces illusions that keep human beings suffering. The belief that other people have the power to take away our happiness denies our responsibility for our own experience. As long as we allow others to determine our well-being, we will be disempowered and the world will remain steeped in agony. It is only when each of us claims responsibility for our experience that we will be free as individuals and empower others as well. I heard about a fellow who was liberated from a Nazi concentration camp by Allied forces at the end of World War II. In contrast to the other frail and downcast survivors, this man looked robust and radiant. Seeing this, the soldiers asked him if he was a newcomer to the camp. No, he replied, he had been one of the longest residents of the place. The difference was his attitude. Horrid though the conditions were, he refused to be defeated by them. His attitude lifted him above suffering. The principle of intention over circumstances was masterfully presented by Viktor Frankl, also a survivor of a Nazi concentration camp, in his classic inspirational book *Man's Search for Meaning*. Later the idea was cleverly dramatized in the movie *Life Is Beautiful*.

The principle of self-responsibility for emotional experience does not give us license to treat each other unkindly. To the contrary, we must make every effort to respect and support each other where we can. Ultimately, however, how someone responds to your actions is their choice, just as how you respond to their actions is your choice. Our true freedom lives in being able to choose the thoughts and attitudes that generate our experience.

When we use money as a tool of love, we soar. When we use money as a tool of punishment, we crash. While many of us hold dear the goal of making money, it is more what we make *of* money that determines our happiness or sorrow.

## THE ANTIDOTE TO FEAR

I coached a woman who had written some excellent diet books to help children with disabilities. Jean had developed a unique diet to improve the health of her own challenged child, with remarkable success. She had completed two books and had a publisher express an interest, but she was hesitating to submit her work. "Why don't you put it out there?" I asked her.

"I feel exposed and vulnerable. What if people don't like my ideas? What if they don't work with other people? What if the books don't sell?"

These are the very questions I often hear from people on the threshold of launching a creative work.

"If you could help one family upgrade their situation and enhance the quality of a child's life, would it be worth it to have your book published?" I asked.

Jean's face lightened. "Of course."

"And if you helped hundreds, or thousands, or millions of people to improve their children's health and happiness, would that outweigh the vulnerability you fear?"

"For sure!"

"And if your contribution generated an income that helped sustain you and your children, would that be a valuable result?"

"Absolutely."

Jean decided to go ahead with her publication. She dissolved her fear about her project by considering its potential for service. This is one of the most powerful shifts I see in clients who are reticent to offer their work to the public. If you have any such anxiety, shift your focus from "What will they think of me?" to "How can this help?" Your fear will dissolve in the face of a higher purpose. As the English proverb goes, "Fear knocked at the door. Faith answered. No one was there."

## THE MYTH:

Putting yourself or your product out there
exposes you and makes you vulnerable.

## THE REALITY:

If you or your product can help one or many people,
the rewards of your offering far exceed the risk you fear.

## WITHHOLDING TAX

Many people withhold love or money (remember, they are the same) because they believe they will be hurt if they give. They believe that their love or money will not be returned. In this case, what hurts is not what you are not receiving. What hurts is what you are not giving. *A Course in Miracles* tells us that in any situation in which you perceive that something is missing, what is missing is what you are not giving. This powerful principle could serve as the meditation of a lifetime.

Consider a situation in which you perceive something to be missing, such as a partner not saying "I love you," or a child misbehaving, or a friend being dishonest. Now consider what you are withholding from this situation. Are you refusing to acknowledge the ways your partner expresses love without words? Might your child's misbehaving be a call for your presence and attention? Have you been entirely honest with your friend? Invest more of yourself in such situations, and two things will happen: (1) You will find the peace you have missed; and (2) The situation will likely change for the better.

## ▨ ▨ MISSING AND GIVING ▨ ▨ ◂

*A situation in which I believe that something is missing:*

_____

_____

*What I believe is missing that someone else is not giving:*

_____

_____

*What may be missing that I have not been giving to this situation:*

_____

_____

*What I could say or do that would indicate my investment to transform this situation:*

_____

_____

*What good, healing, or resolution could come to me if I gave what I have not been giving:*

_____

_____

*What good, healing, or resolution could come for the other person(s) if I gave what I have not been giving:*

_____

_____

Now take an action step to transform this situation by giving something new, different, or more.

■ ■ ■

It is said, "Giving 100 percent is easy. Giving 99 percent is difficult." What burdens us is our resistance and holding back because we are afraid. Face the fear, drop the resistance, infuse love, and the issue will resolve. Norman Vincent Peale, author of the classic *The Power of Positive Thinking*, advised, "Be an all-out, not a hold-out." The goal of giving is not to get. The goal of giving is to reap the joy of giving, which far exceeds the joy of getting. To give *is* to get. When we establish our work in authentic service, all kinds of wonderful things come to us that we would never enjoy if we were focused on getting only.

One of my Life Coach Training graduates was struggling with whether or not to devote himself to his coaching career. He was going back and forth on his commitment and getting mediocre results with his clients and income. Then he reported, "I decided to really do it. Now I am all in." From that point his coaching practice took off and he became one of our most successful graduates. The turning point came when he decided to give 100 percent. What was hurting him was not what he was not receiving. What was hurting him was what he was not giving. When he gave all, he got all.

---

## THE MYTH:
You can give less than all and get all.

## THE REALITY:
To get all you must give all.

---

Illusions twist truth to make black appear white, and white appear black. They promise that if you take without giving, you will get what you want. Fear not that if you give more and demand less, you will fall short. Life finds ingenious ways to support those who support others. A minister told me, "I never worry about money because my finances are founded on universal principles." At some point you must decide if you will trust the intelligence that created and sustains the universe, or the story of lack you have learned that replaces it. That decision becomes obvious when you consider how well your current story is working. If you feel any anxiety about money or business, or that you must gather as much as you can to protect yourself, or that you must take something from someone else to improve your position, you will recognize that the ego's plan has not delivered as promised. Under the spotlight of expanded vision, it becomes clear that giving is not the opposite of receiving. It is the very key to receiving.

---

## TRUTH #7
## GENEROSITY IS THE ROYAL ROAD TO RICHES

---

# ILLUSION #8:
# COMPETITION IS HEALTHY AND REQUIRED

On a warm moonlit night on the idyllic island of Saint John in the Caribbean, a friend and I decided to go for a swim. As we made our way through the jungle toward the beach, I heard scratching sounds beside the path. Quickly I grabbed my flashlight and shined it into the bush. There I beheld a weird sight: a massive cluster of huge land crabs were climbing over each other to get to something on the base of a tree. As I watched several dozen of these alien-looking creatures clawing and crawling their way toward the apex of the writhing mound, it occurred to me that this is how many people approach their business: *I must fight my way to the top of the heap. I will step on anyone who gets in my way and use them for leverage. Emerging as number one is the supreme achievement.*

Then we wonder why we are in pain, why we don't enjoy satisfying relationships, and why we never seem to have enough or be enough. We see business as a constant battle for trophies just beyond our reach, attainable only by conquering competitors. Our career becomes a real-life version of the *Survivor* television series as we are pitted against everyone else on the island for the single prize. Their loss becomes our gain. Only one top dog survives and triumphs.

Few people stop to consider the insanity of such a system or their participation in it. Sanity, by contrast, reveals that no God in its right mind would create such a ruthless world. Only people steeped in the illusion of separateness, motivated by fear, would engender such a cruel realm and dwell in it.

The day comes when each of us can no longer tolerate the angst that such misguided beliefs engender, and we seek a way out. Competition is not the will of our Creator, and you are not required to labor under it. An escape hatch is available—if you are ready to use it.

## RISE ABOVE THE FRAY

When I interview contractors to promote my business, candidates usually ask me, "Who is your competition?" I laugh when I hear that question. I answer, "I don't have any competition. The people who do work similar to mine are my good friends. I respect them and they respect me. They attract the people who are a fit for them, and I attract the people who are a fit for me. There are plenty of customers out there, enough to sustain all of us."

That perspective sounds odd, even crazy, in a world in which competition seems so real and necessary and drives the greater part of business strategy. Yet if you are going to prosper beyond your current level, you must examine long-standing beliefs and decide if they are valid and if you wish to found your work and life on them. Many traditional beliefs are more limiting than liberating. They need to be either upleveled or discarded.

The belief in competition is a classic example of horizontal thinking: There are a fixed amount of resources—in this case, customers and their money—for which you must vie to gain your share. Vertical thinking, by contrast, reminds you that there are plenty of people who can benefit from your product or service, they can find their way to you, and they will be happy to pay you for your help.

Here are seven ways to rise above the competition fray:

## 1. Recognize the uniqueness of your product or service.

You have something unusual that can serve the world in a way that others don't. Even if you are marketing a commonly used product or service, you embody qualities that others don't. Let's say you are a massage therapist in a city where massage therapists abound. Everywhere you turn you see posters, magazine ads, and business cards advertising massage therapy. You may feel daunted when you consider how many therapists are doing what you do and vying for the clients you seek. If you become immersed in thoughts of scarcity, you may limp along, lower your prices, resort to desperate, expensive, or silly promotions, or give up. But there is another way to think about your profession that transforms the playing field. Anyone can massage a client, but the way *you* do it is unique to your personality, energy, and intentions. If you truly care about your clients and want them to have a positive experience, they will be drawn to you not so much for the way you move your hands, but because of the person behind them. I have received massages from many different therapists. Most of them were okay, but just a few stand out because I experienced those therapists' full presence, caring, comforting touch, and intention for my well-being. I return to those few again and again because they match the experience I seek.

The more you are true to your unique preferences and talents, the more you will attract clients who recognize and value them, and are happy to pay you for them. If you believe you have to mimic someone else, adopt a style that runs contrary to your joy, or compromise your standards, you set yourself up for frustration and failure. Emerson said, "Imitation is suicide." We may not commit physical suicide, but we commit spiritual suicide when we deny who we are in order to be accepted. We can conversely say, "Authenticity is sustenance."

## 2. Give the gift of life.

You are not just offering a mechanical product or service. The aliveness you exude magnetizes your clients, co-workers, and others involved with your success. Even more than customers seek a particular product, they are yearning for life force. Most people are disconnected from their passion. They lead busy, overwhelming, and often empty or meaningless lives. When they meet someone who is genuinely connected to vitality, they feel lifted and inspired by your presence. Through the vehicle of your product or service, your customers are energized and attracted to work with you. Everyone has a built-in "passion meter" that lights up in the presence of a human being who radiates life force. Stay true to your passion and you will attract clients for reasons that go beyond your product or service.

---

## THE MYTH:
The actions you take determine your success.

## THE REALITY:
The energy behind your actions determines your success.

---

## 3. Give your customers world-class service.

Only a small percentage of businesses go the distance. If you deliver maximum quality, you will shine in a class by yourself. Rather than competing with others, keep raising the bar on what you offer. The secret to achieving this is simple but takes commitment: More than anything else, want your customers to be happy with what you do for them. When you find reward in their joy, they will recognize your intention and flock to work with you and pay you.

I sometimes present seminars at the Four Seasons Hotel on Maui. This upscale resort charges a minimum $500 for a room and up to $20,000 for a suite per night. When I last spoke there, the spa manager told me that the hotel's 400 rooms and suites were completely sold out for the holidays. The food and spa services are also extremely expensive. I used to wonder how the hotel gets so many people to pay so much money for lodging and amenities that they could get elsewhere for a lower cost. The answer, I discovered, is that the employees are exceptionally well trained to take impeccable care of the guests. From the desk clerks to the chambermaids, to the waiters, to the lifeguards, the staff makes every guest feel welcome and honored like royalty. They address all the guests by name, smile, are courteous, and do all they can to please the customers. Then, of course, there are the luxurious facilities. People are willing to pay a lot to be treated kindly and professionally.

Note: You can't make believe your first priority is to take care of your customers if your first priority is to make money from them. While some people can be fooled, there is a place inside every human being that recognizes sincere caring. Touch the part of your clients that knows quality. Deliver to them that level of service and they will regard you as a rare find and be loyal to you.

## 4. Establish your own market.

The iPod, iPhone, and iPad did not exist before Apple came up with those inventions. Now most people and businesses feel they can't live without them or their imitators. Most consumers own multiple devices, and many upgrade whenever the latest and greatest model is released. Airlines now issue iPads to pilots rather than have them fly with weighty paper manuals. Hotels station tablets throughout the facility to guide guests. Restaurants use wireless gadgets to send orders to the kitchen. They are everywhere! If Steve Jobs and Apple sat around trying to figure out how to build a better PC, the company would not be what it is today. Instead of grappling horizontally, they went vertical and are thriving in unprecedented ways. The Apple computer is an entirely different animal than the PC. You have to think differently to use it because its inventors thought differently to create it.

I love the expression "Come into your own." We usually say this about a young person who has been searching or struggling and then finds a comfortable niche in which his or her talents shine. To succeed maximally, you must step fully into your own self and your own visions. After my Life Coach Training students go through about two months of their practice coaching sessions, a good number of them report, "This is what I was born to do!" There is something *you* were born to do, or at least do for now. This feels like coming home because it is a pure statement of your unique self.

If you have not found your niche yet, don't despair. You are in your perfect position according to your unique path. Every step is important and leads to places you cannot imagine now. Extract the riches and blessings right where you stand, and those rewarding feelings will lead you to what is yours.

---

*Because you do not compete,*
*you will not have competition.*

— Lao Tse, *Tao Te Ching*

---

## 5. Quit keeping score.

If you are busy comparing your product's ranking on Amazon or counting how many people attended your competitor's webinar, you will get dragged away from your true goal, which is to reach the people who match you, or your "just right tribe." Shoot for five-star ratings not because they exceed your competitor's four stars, but because five stars means you are reaching and satisfying your audience. Be the best at what *you* do, not what your competitor does.

If you look at what your competitors are doing, do so only to learn from them and improve your offering. Glean lessons from their mistakes and put their good ideas to use. Examine your product reviews for the same reason. Your real relationships are between you and yourself, your clients, and God, not between you and your competition. In the spiritual dimension, competition is meaningless and does not exist. Only the ego has invented the idea and experience of competition, and is not the least bit worth indulging.

---

*Comparison is the thief of joy.*

— Mark Twain

---

> # THE MYTH:
> If you are doing better than your competitors, you win.
>
> # THE REALITY:
> If you are fulfilling your potential, you win.

## 6. Don't count the house.

Just as you want to reach the right clients who match you, you want to reach the right number of clients who match you. I don't pray or intend for a particular number of clients. I pray for the clients who can benefit from my services and whom I enjoy working with. Sometimes the numbers are higher and sometimes they are lower. I trust that the providence principle is organizing my signups. I am not responsible for who shows up or how many; that is Spirit's department. I am responsible to let people know what I am offering and then take good care of them when they arrive. I don't have to worry about paying my bills. When I need more money, more customers show up. This is an amazing process to observe and participate in.

Robert and Barbara Varley traveled around the country in a small van, teaching *A Course in Miracles* seminars in many cities, on a donation basis. One December their van broke down and they determined that they needed a new one. The couple went to a local dealership and selected a new vehicle. When the time came to close the deal, their inner guidance told them not to haggle, but to just pay the asking price. When they did, the salesman came to tears. He told the couple that Christmas was coming and he didn't know how he would pay for presents for his children. His commission from this sale would help him do that. During the next few months, the income from the Varleys' seminars swelled hugely, enabling them to pay off the van. Then it dropped back to its previous level. They realized that Higher Power was guiding the entire process, and the series of events was a pathway for miracles.

### 7. Connect with your customers.

The technology explosion has enabled many companies to find ways to avoid direct contact with customers. They expect all interactions to occur online and don't even offer a telephone number for customers to contact the company. Some companies offer a phone number, but when customers reach the company, they have access only to automated recordings and can hardly, if ever, get to a human being.

While this method saves the company time and money, it removes the human element in business, which is the lifeblood of success. Sacrificing person-to-person interaction for the sake of the bottom line paves the road to self-sabotage. A Jewish friend of mine went to the airport to pick up a revered rabbi who was to give a presentation at the local synagogue. As the two were driving toward the exit of the airport parking lot, my friend was trying to decide whether to go through an automatic toll payment lane or a lane staffed by a person. The rabbi told my friend, "Let's go through the lane with a person. The Creator gave us each other to enjoy relationships, and we must never miss the opportunity to connect."

In my Life Coach Training, I recommend various technical aids for the coaches, including a good headset for coaching via telephone. Because I have had a very positive experience with a particular company (Headsets.com), I recommend that the coaches explore their products. I phoned the company to find out if they had some kind of affiliate program for distribution of their products. The next day I received a phone call from the company's CEO, who informed me that they did not have such a program, but he would be happy to send me a complimentary gift of their most expensive product as a way of thanking me for promoting their company. I found this to be a very classy act, not just for the generous gift, but for the CEO reaching out to connect with me directly. This bolstered my support for the company in my trainings and netted the company more profits in the long run.

Many companies outsource their customer service agent positions in order to save money. Why pay someone in this country $12 an hour when you can pay someone in Asia $2? Economically, the move makes sense. This works only if the quality of service and communication between the company and client holds up. Clients who get an agent whose English they cannot understand, or who is speaking via a poor telephone connection, are likely to go elsewhere next time. If you are going to cut costs, make sure you maintain a high standard of customer service. Consider how you would like to be treated if you were a customer seeking help from your company. The better you take care of your clients, the better they will take care of you.

## BUSINESS WITHOUT VIOLENCE

Many expressions in business reflect a mind-set of war and violence:

"He made a killing in the stock market."

"That deal was a real coup."

"We are undergoing a hostile takeover."

"Will we meet the deadline?"

"How much market share did we capture?"

"That campaign kicked ass."

"What a killer presentation!"

"This product is priced aggressively."

"The CEO took a lot of flak."

"HR was the biggest casualty in the merger."

"Take no prisoners in this price war."

"That strategy will put us in a financial minefield."

"The company has a stranglehold on the local market."

"When the boss gets back, heads are going to roll."

"A hundred employees got sacked."

"The company went belly up."

Reading a business newspaper or magazine can be like going through a war novel. And if you're tired of fictional shoot-'em-ups, you can bone up on these popular how-to books on business success:

*Rules of the Hunt*

*Victory Secrets of Attila the Hun*

*Swim with the Sharks without Being Eaten Alive*

*The Sociopath Next Door*

*The No Asshole Rule*

*Working with You is Killing Me*

*The Bully-Free Workplace: Stop Jerks, Weasels, and Snakes from Killing Your Organization*

*Mobbing: Emotional Abuse in the American Workplace*

*Nice Girls Don't Get the Corner Office*

*Never Split the Difference: Negotiating As If Your Life Depended on It*

*The Art of War* is Amazon.com's #1 bestseller in religious philosophy. It seems odd that war is the most popular subject for people interested in religion, which generally stands for creating peace. But no one said the world is logical. *A Course in Miracles* tells us that the values of the world are the precise opposite of the values of heaven. Likewise, the world of business is supposed to make people's lives easier, but in many cases it expands the very battlefield we are trying to escape.

Even business attire is based on warfare. The necktie, a traditional requirement for men in formal business situations, derives from a scarf that medieval knights donned when they went into combat. Neckties offer no benefit besides meeting a social expectation, and they choke you. The first thing men do when they get out of the office or come home from work is remove their necktie. *Thank goodness the struggles of the day are over. Now I can relax until I get back onto the battlefield tomorrow.*

If you are tired of going to war every day, you may be ready to reframe your job and see it as a playing field rather than a battlefield. Other people can choose to turn their day into a tug-of-war if they wish, but you don't need to join them. In the engaging movie *Holy Man*, Eddie Murphy portrays a humble spiritual teacher named "G." G has such terrific charisma that masses of people fall in love with him, are inspired by every word he utters, and buy anything he recommends. A struggling salesman sees G as his chance to save his floundering career by exploiting G's charm to sell his products. G goes along with the scheme, not to get anything for himself, but to help this pathetic fellow. Even while G is thrown into the fray of frenzied sales, he never loses his inner peace or his winning smile. Greedy execs stoop to unethical antics around G, but he cannot be moved. In the end, his purity triumphs, and he transforms the people he touches. Competition never once entered his mind. All he wanted to do was help where he could.

## THE MYTH:

Business requires conflict, violence, and domination.

## THE REALITY:

Conscious business is founded in ethical
practices, mutual support, and cooperation.

## A HIGHER USE FOR COMPETITION

While competition is generally ego-driven, the Higher Mind can take the ego's invention and employ it for positive purposes. Rather than competing with other people or companies, compete with yourself. Stretch beyond old limits and conquer the territory of uncharted excellence. Instead of vanquishing business foes, defeat the villains of fear, doubt, and suffocating illusions. Mobilize your greater self to overcome any sense of littleness. To your inmost spirit, such a defeat is meaningless, since that self prevails simply by being itself, and does not need an enemy to trounce. But if you must be competitive, make the propensity work toward a healthy goal at no one's loss.

Lesson 133 of *A Course in Miracles* asks us to affirm, "I will not value what is valueless." In this lesson the Course lays out various criteria for us to make decisions that will net us the most joy and success in life. One of those criteria states that if your gain requires someone else to lose, it is no gain at all. When you give a material gift, the giver has less and the recipient has more. When you give a spiritual gift, such as kindness, forgiveness, or healing, both the giver and the receiver gain. Thus ends the win-lose model under which humanity has suffered for millennia.

While the ego defines itself by battle, the Spirit within us founds its power in simply being what it is. While a part of your mind is immersed in various conflicts, another part of you (the real you) is established in perfect peace. The journey to success is based not on winning wars, but in transferring your attention, allegiance, and experience to the part of you already absorbed in well-being. Enlightenment is not a change of behavior. It is a shift of awareness.

---

## THE MYTH:

You are in competition with other people or companies.

## THE REALITY:

If you must compete, defeat your fears, limits, and illusions.

---

## CROSSING THE FINISH LINE TOGETHER

A remarkable event once occurred at the Special Olympics. During a foot race, one of the runners stumbled and fell down on the track. When the other contestants saw him drop, they stopped and helped him to his feet. The entire group locked arms, continued together, and crossed the finish line all at the same time. To a competitor, such an act is unthinkable—why stop to help someone else if that will impede you from winning? Yet to a person of conscience, helping someone else *is* winning. Those Special Olympians, while judged by the world as disabled, were fully abled in heart, which gives us pause to consider what constitutes real achievement.

I used to work with the population that participated in the Special Olympics. I staffed a sheltered workshop for people with severe mental disabilities. Though physically adults, these people had the innocent minds of very young children. They had no sense of proving themselves, competing, or earning a living. They were immersed in just being. The sponsors of the organization tried to justify the program by giving the participants simple contract jobs, like stuffing a small plastic tube into a cork that would be sold as part of a fish tank. The organizers were trying to turn this population into "normal" citizens, which was never going to happen. These people were who they were, and normality was not on their curriculum for this lifetime. The clients couldn't care less about earning a penny per tube, or a dollar, or any sum. They simply wanted to interact with each other, laugh, sing, and eat. While my job was challenging and I recognized the intense difficulties that caring for such special-needs individuals posed to their families and the community, I found their innocence refreshing. They were not encumbered with the complex intellects with which many of us attempt to navigate our lives, hyperanalysis that often burdens us to the point of depression, burnout, and illness. For this go-round these people had chosen a different path of learning—and teaching. They modeled a kind of freedom that, if we applied it, could enable us to escape the insane pressures to succeed under which we labor.

## THE MYTH:
One person wins at the expense of others, who are losers.

## THE REALITY:
When we keep our values in order, everyone wins.

## WHEN THE LEADING EDGE BECOMES THE BLEEDING EDGE

Some people argue that competition brings out the best in us. It forces us to dig in, sharpen our skills, and excel. This is so if you have such a high value on winning that competition motivates you to do the work to pluck the prize.

People who are sincerely dedicated to mastering their craft do not need to measure themselves against others in order to grow. They are moved to excel for the sheer joy of excelling. They don't need others to challenge them because they challenge themselves. Their journey of success develops from the inside out rather than between people. Great musicians, for example, don't need to enter musical competitions to hone their skills. They push themselves not to defeat a foe, but to create soaring melodies. Genuine masters are motivated purely by self-fulfillment.

Taken to an extreme, competition debilitates the competitor. I saw a documentary about an Olympic swimmer who was obsessed with winning a gold medal. His entire life was about training and winning. This fellow was not a happy camper. He was driven to the point of severe neurosis and had virtually no life other than swimming. When he finally got to the Olympics, he won a silver medal. This "loss" pushed him to train even more rigorously. Four years later he did win a gold medal, which gave him a momentary huge rush. Then he was back training to compete again in the following Olympic games. While I admire this athlete for his discipline, determination, and perseverance, the quality of his life was severely diminished. He missed years of now moments for the one hoped-for moment of victory. If happiness is the true measure of success, he was not very successful. He won the Olympic gold, but missed the inner gold. Any medal you can hold in your hand is not nearly as valuable as the fulfillment you hold in your heart.

---

### THE MYTH:
One moment of victory is worth years
or a lifetime of struggle.

### THE REALITY:
The ongoing quality of your life is far more
important than any single event.

---

## OUR TRUE NATURE

"Just look at nature," some might argue. "It's all based on competition and survival of the fittest. The bigger animal devours the smaller animal, and the strongest gorilla is alpha of the troop. He eats first and has his choice of females to mate with. If you deny competition, you will be overrun by aggressive people seeking to dominate you."

This is so if you believe that human beings are animals only. If that were true, we are subject only to the law of the jungle, and only bullies prevail. Yet there is an aspect of humanity that elevates us above the law of the jungle. We are imbued with a higher nature founded on an entirely different set of laws than those that rule the jungle. Because most people are disconnected from their spiritual source, a lot of what happens on the planet is just another day in the jungle. Yet there are people who recognize their innate divinity and strive to live by it. They realize that while our bodies have jungle tendencies, our deeper nature is godly.

Temple Grandin is an extraordinary woman who grew up autistic, with heightened sensitivity that caused her to feel the pain of mistreated animals. As a result, she has become a world-respected advocate for ethical treatment of livestock, and has invented apparatuses to diminish the suffering of cattle. (I recommend her biopic *Temple Grandin*.) Grandin noted, "Just because nature is cruel, we don't have to be." *A Course in Miracles* calls us to remember, "There is no cruelty in God and none in me."

This statement certainly seems antithetical to the events we watch on the news. Lots of people do very cruel things and hurt many people. You and I have acted cruelly as well, purposely or inadvertently. Yet the Course is pointing to a deeper reality: While we may be tempted to do cruel things, or do, cruelty is not our nature. At our core we are loving, kind, and angelic. We engage in cruel acts because we have become seduced by fear-based illusions. A person who hurts someone is wounded. Hurt people hurt people. It takes a victim to make a victim. If you were to strip away the painful experiences that cause a cruel person to act out antisocial behaviors, you would find the innocent being he or she was before that person learned to fear and hate. Our inherent nature is love. All else is a distraction or aberration.

While competition and conquering may be commonplace, cooperation is far more natural. I was a guest on a radio interview along with Dr. Wayne Dyer and a famous yoga teacher. The yoga teacher proudly announced that he was sponsoring a world yoga competition. Hearing that, Wayne's forehead wrinkled and he commented, "I thought yoga was about cooperation, not competition." The ego takes anything it finds, including things innocent, and turns it into a competition. The word "yoga" means "joining together." To introduce the idea of competition into yoga is to refute the origin, nature, and purpose of yoga. Most good yoga teachers advise during a class, "Don't look around the room to see what other people are doing and compare yourself to them. Simply strive to achieve your ideal. Don't beat yourself up if you do not execute the pose perfectly. Be kind to yourself as you practice and progress."

We all seek to be true to ourselves. But before you can be true to yourself, you must know what your real self is. "Who am I?" is the most important question to answer in your life, the ultimate goal of all human endeavor and inquiry. All enlightened beings, from every religion and spiritual tradition, tell us that we are far more than our bodies, cultural conditioning, and jungle tendencies. The truth about us is that we are divine. Everything we do leads us to that fundamental knowing.

---

## THE MYTH:

Humanity is inherently cruel.
The world is ruled by the law of the jungle.

## THE REALITY:

Humanity is inherently divine.
Higher laws supersede a jungle mentality.

---

## HEALING COMPETITION AT ITS CORE

Competition in the workplace is but the tip of the iceberg of competition that has pervaded the history of humanity. Business competition is the least violent of the battles humankind has waged. Millions of people have been killed and vast domains plundered by tyrants and nations competing for territory, natural resources, and political domination. Even more tragically, more people have been killed in religious wars and inquisitions than in political conflicts. People fight and kill over romantic interests. Parents at Little League baseball games get into brawls, bashing parents of competing teams with their lawn chairs. A mind steeped in competition can find any object to claim as "mine" and attempt to destroy those who threaten it.

All sports are based on competition. From the most violent sports such as boxing, wrestling, and football, to far gentler rivalries like golf, chess, and spelling bees, the theme is the same: one or more individuals are pitted against each other, vying for a title or prize; one contestant will emerge victorious by defeating the others.

While sports are competitive, they serve the positive function of sublimating base brutal instincts. Football players pounding and tackling each other give teams and fans a relatively safe outlet for violent impulses they might otherwise use to kill each other on streets or battlefields. Moving kings, queens, bishops, and knights around on a chessboard gently symbolizes maneuvering such entities in wars between kingdoms. Olympic athletes throw the javelin and shot put, weapons of war in ancient times. The high jump and pole vault were originally used to infiltrate enemy strongholds. The fastest runner caught the prey or escaped the predator. Sports serve as a safety valve to offset greater harm.

To move to the next level collectively, we must shine the light on the competition in which we each engage individually. Do you feel compelled to get to the one available parking space before the car coming down the road takes it? Do you jockey for power to control decisions in your relationship? Do you grow worried or jealous that someone will take your lover away? Do you feel like a failure if you are not in the top 10 percent of your class? If you play in a band, theater troupe, or other performance ensemble, do you vie to be the star? How important is it to you that you win an argument? How much integrity are you willing to sacrifice to get something that lots of people want? Several years ago a mob of shoppers tore into a department store at its 5 A.M. Black Friday opening and trampled a pregnant woman to death in the rampage. If ever there was evidence that we need to take charge of our competitive instincts, this incident is it.

While you and I may not be able to control the decisions of our country, religion, or crazed shoppers, we *are* able to steer our personal choices. If we can recognize where we participate in competition and conquest, and do what we can to replace such acts with cooperation and mutual support, we take important steps to transform our world. While we exert some influence with our political vote, we exert greater influence by the way we conduct our lives.

## IDENTIFYING COMPETITIVE TENDENCIES

Check the boxes that indicate the areas of your life in which you tend to compete:

- ❏ *I compete in business with other companies.*
- ❏ *I compete with people within my company.*
- ❏ *I am very competitive in sports.*
- ❏ *I believe that my political party is superior to the opposition.*
- ❏ *I compare my body and looks to others.*

❏  *I compare my income and other symbols of success with others.*

❏  *I feel smarter or dumber than other people.*

❏  *I try to get to a parking space before someone else does.*

❏  *I believe that my religion is better than others or the only way to heaven.*

❏  *I feel proud when my grades are higher than others and self-critical if they are less.*

❏  *I take a certain satisfaction in being ahead of others in a line.*

❏  *I judge my relationship partner in comparison to others.*

❏  *I am glad that I am [younger] [older] than others.*

❏  *I argue to convince others that I am right and they are wrong.*

❏  *I enjoy watching sports, dramas, war movies, or game shows in which people or groups are battling one another.*

Any other competitive tendencies you notice:

_____

_____

_____

⬛  ⬛  ⬛

The first step to transcend competition is to become aware of it and the results it accrues. If the competitions in which you engage bring you joy and soul satisfaction, they are serving you well. Competition that springs from fear, lack, and separation undermines the human spirit. Let go of forms of competition that drag you down, and replace them with activities that uplift you and support others.

## GAME CHANGERS

A growing number of individuals and companies are breaking free of the conquest mentality and offering models of cooperation. Tesla Motors is revolutionizing the auto industry by producing inexpensive, efficient, attractive, and comfortable all-electric cars. CEO Elon Musk has refused to patent the company's engineering technology. Any company is free to copy and use the Tesla design. Musk is more interested in bringing sustainable technology to the planet than in hogging the profits for himself or his company. Meanwhile Tesla is soaring. During a recent economic quarter, Tesla was the highest-valued stock in the auto industry.

There is a growing movement in the software industry to offer open-source applications, free to anyone who wishes to use them. WordPress, for example, is an extremely popular website design application used by millions of developers free of charge. The designers of this program and its many plug-ins simply request donations from those who use them. Likewise, Wikipedia, the world's largest online repository of reference information, is available to everyone at no charge, without any advertising, functioning entirely on donations from appreciative users.

---

### THE MYTH:

Possessing and protecting secrets and commodities gives you or your company the leading edge.

### THE REALITY:

Sharing useful knowledge and resources prospers you, your company, and society.

---

I saw a video in which a 10-year-old boy, sitting in the bleachers of a major league baseball game, caught a home run ball in his baseball glove. Sitting next to him was a younger boy who missed catching the ball and broke into tears when the older boy caught it instead. Seeing the child's reaction, the older boy tossed the ball to the younger kid as his own prize.

In another inspiring account, a fellow purchased an antique dresser for a small price at an auction. When he took the piece home, he discovered a hidden compartment in one of the drawers containing a cache of diamonds, jewelry, and currency worth thousands of dollars. Instead of invoking "finders, keepers," he contacted the auctioneer, who returned the treasure to the unknowing original owners who had inherited the dresser from a relative.

These are just a few examples of individuals who, even for a moment, rose beyond the competition mentality that has kept the world in chains. While we all have competitive tendencies, we also have the capacity to work together rather than against each other. Such cooperative moments open windows to heaven, illuminating the pathway to humanity's highest potential.

## THRIVAL OF THE FITTEST

The maxim "survival of the fittest" conjures images of the biggest, strongest, toughest lion in the jungle—"king of the beasts." Many people act like beasts attempting to bully their way through business. If you meet them on their terms, you indulge and perpetuate savage tendencies. But there is a nobler ground you can meet them on that will potentiate their higher nature and yours. When Pontius Pilate interrogated Jesus, "Are you the king of the Jews?" he answered, "My kingdom is not of this world." Jesus was affirming that there was a far vaster realm that he lived in, not subject to the politics and petty squabbles the world holds dear. That broader domain is available to all of us. Every time you and I step into our office, answer a customer's request, or negotiate a contract, we must ask ourselves the same question: What kingdom do I prefer to live in?

If you are going to succeed at "survival of the fittest," define fitness as doing what works best in any given situation. Those who know how to fit in prevail beyond those who attempt to dominate. Many creatures survive because they blend in with the environment. *Tao Te Ching* teaches that humility and the ability to flow are the salient strengths of authentic leaders. Rigidness and force weaken leadership and undermine success. What is aligned with the Tao thrives, and what is not aligned perishes. This dynamic puts an entirely different spin on your business decisions. What would humility guide you to do that force would overlook? How might harmony be preferable to victory? When is it time to speak up and act, and when is it time to remain silent? An entirely more empowering level of alignment with the natural order is available to you. When you tap into it, you are truly the fittest, and you will not only survive, but thrive.

## STEPPING INTO THE NEW PARADIGM

We stand at the threshold of upending the belief in competition as a necessity or asset to our lives. While much of humanity remains steeped in comparison and conflict, a small group is choosing to walk off the battlefield and stand in the light. Let's remember the group of Slovakian protesters whose photo I mentioned earlier. Gathered in a city square facing a brigade of policemen clad in riot gear, the protestors simply stood quietly with their eyes closed, praying and meditating. Their silence was thunderous. If you are tired of fighting for your good or pitting yourself against others, you are a part of the band of revolutionaries that may more appropriately be called evolutionaries. The idea of revolution implies warfare in which the new triumphs over the old. Evolution, by contrast, implies that what no longer works gives way to what serves better. The snake sheds the old skin when the sheath has outlived its purpose, and a new, healthier skin grows in its place. There is no fight, just a natural progression. You don't have to battle the useless. You just have to practice the useful.

The world you and I were born into is not the world we live in now, and tomorrow's world will take us to places we cannot even imagine. We are not climbing a mountain; we are flowing on a river. English physicist, astronomer, and mathematician Sir James Jeans declared, "Science should leave off making pronouncements: the river of knowledge has too often turned back on itself." So it is with business. While competition seems to be a given reality, it is we who have given it. The same mind that conjured conflict can escape from it. Like the Special Olympians who chose a shared victory rather than an individual one, we too can garner a new kind of trophy that signals greater life for all.

## TRUTH #8
## COOPERATION AND MUTUAL SUPPORT YIELD THE HIGHEST SUCCESS

# ILLUSION #9:
# THE RULES OF BUSINESS ARE AN EXCEPTION TO THE LAWS OF LIFE

I was excited about my invitation to present a program for a prestigious company's top-producing sales force—until I checked their website. The corporation was immersed in worldwide oil and military contracts, the very enterprises I marched against in college. But the company wanted me to teach their employees how to create a healthy work/life balance, a goal I feel passionate about and with which I could help them. So I accepted.

Feeling anxious about the presentation, I phoned my friend Dr. Robert Holden, a holistically oriented trainer who has advised many top corporations and presented popular BBC and PBS documentaries. When I asked Robert if he had any advice about my program, he gave me an enigmatic response: "There is no such thing as business." What a strange statement from someone who earns his living by helping businesses grow! Since that day I have given his statement considerable thought, and I will decipher it for you later in this chapter. Robert concluded his advice with, "Just do what you usually do and you will be fine."

But I didn't heed his guidance. Instead, I did what many people do when faced with presentation anxiety—I retreated to PowerPoint, one of the leading causes of death by boredom in the corporate world. I abandoned my heart, took refuge in my intellect, and planned like crazy. This was not healthy planning. It was neurotic, which always works *against* a goal. Over weeks of preparation I stuffed a glut of graphs, illustrations, and a few video clips into the presentation.

The day of the presentation came, and the super-salespeople, CEO, and other high-level execs marched into the hotel ballroom. As I began to click through my slides, I realized that the talk was dry, intellectual, and inauthentic. I was trying too hard, hurtling toward a train wreck. I glanced at the CEO in the front row, sitting with his arms crossed, obviously bored and disappointed. *Don't worry*, I told myself, *it will all be over soon.*

I came to the last 15 minutes of the presentation, during which I had planned a few short experiential exercises. I asked everyone to stand and find three people they appreciated, and express to each one specifically what they were grateful for. The moment I issued that instruction, a chill of fear rippled through the room, as if I had asked these people to take off their clothes and parade nude. The entire group sat stunned and saucer-eyed, like deer hypnotized by auto headlights. But, obedient performers that they were, they forced themselves to rise and participate. After a minute the somber tone that had pervaded the room shifted to amiable chatter. Then the volume rose, accompanied by laughter. After a few minutes the upbeat energy amplified exponentially, filling the space with joyful, vibrant interaction, punctuated by raucous exclamations. The group was having a grand time, totally immersed in the exercise. They were having so much fun that I had to practically yell to corral them back to their seats. The contrast between the dry lecture and the experiential exercise was staggering.

As soon as the presentation was over, the CEO approached me and shook my hand vigorously. "That was fantastic!" he said. "We've never done anything like that before. Everyone loved it!" Then he lowered his tone and confessed, "I have to admit I was worried during the PowerPoint section. But this exercise put the presentation over the top. This was the best program we have ever had. We want you back again next year!"

As I drove home, I wondered if I had delivered the program more for the participants' education or for my own. The insight I gained was rock solid: People in the corporate world deeply crave connection. They have had enough PowerPoint for many lifetimes. Workers are starving for human contact. When they get it, amazing things happen.

## UNIVERSAL PRINCIPLES EVERYWHERE

Many of us have been trained to believe that what makes business work is somehow different from what makes life work. In life we are taught to love our neighbor, be generous, and pull together for the common good. When we arrive at the office, however, such benevolent ideals fly out the window. It's dog-eat-dog, devour the competition, get rid of anyone who stands in your way, profits before people, and so on. We are told, "All's fair in love and war." Since many people consider business a form of war, they believe that all is also fair in business. But why would we expect to find happiness in business via a different route than we would find happiness in life? Is business really a unique quadrant in which separate rules apply? Let's explore why the foundation upon which all of life is built is the foundation upon which successful business is built.

### 1. Every act is a choice between fear and love.

*A Course in Miracles* teaches that there are only two fundamental human emotions and experiences: love and fear. All other emotions are derivatives of these two. If it's not love, it's fear. Love in this context does not refer simply to romance, sex, or huggy, touchy-feely, mushy interactions. It refers to the experience of profound well-being, exuberant aliveness, and connection to our deep inner Source. Expressions of love include creativity, joy, trust, inspired vision, and a sincere desire to serve. The derivatives of fear include a sense of separation, competition, defensiveness, need to control, conflict, and accumulation for self at the expense of others. Which of the two above descriptions more accurately describes the world of business as we have created it? If you agree that business is more often steeped in fear, you can see why and where we have our homework to do.

Acts that proceed from fear always backfire. When that happens, you must return to the crossroads where you chose other than love and make a different choice. If you consider the actions in your life that have led to some kind of trouble, you will see that you made a fear-based decision that resulted in pain for you or others. Yet those experiences were not in vain; ultimately, they taught you to make new decisions from a higher mind-set. As you master this skill, those past experiences, while distressing at the time, prove to be crucial stepping-stones to your evolution.

## THE MYTH:
Fear-based actions will get you the results you desire.

## THE REALITY:
Fear-based actions backfire. Integrity-based actions get you what you want and need.

Let's take a moment now to recognize how *all* of your experiences, both joyful and painful, help you learn to discern between the voices of love and fear and then make healthier choices.

## ■ ■ ■ THE CRUCIAL CHOICE ■ ■ ■

*An action I took that was motivated by fear, and how it backfired:*

_____

_____

*What I learned from that experience that helps me in the long run:*

_____

_____

*An action I took based on love that worked, and what happened as a result:*

_____

_____

*A decision before me now:*

_____

_____

*What the voice of fear tells me to do:*

_____

_____

*What the voice of love tells me to do:*

_____

_____

*One action step I can take to follow and express the higher voice:*

_____

_____

## 2. Healthy relationships form the building blocks of a successful business.

Denise has managed a thriving corporate department for over two decades. During the last 14 years, she has worked closely with her supervisor, Troy. When Denise decided to branch out into life coaching as a second career, she told Troy that she would not be able to offer as much overtime work as she had been doing. Denise concluded, "I hope this won't affect our relationship."

To Denise's surprise, Troy stoically replied, "I didn't know we had a relationship."

Denise was floored. It was amazing to her that this man with whom she had interacted so intensively for so many years was unaware he had a relationship with her.

Relationships are the foundational component of business. To minimize or overlook them is professional suicide. If you want your business to flourish, honor and support the people who make the business thrive. When all is said and done, it is our human connections that give our life and work meaning and value. No one on their deathbed wishes they had spent more time in the office. Instead, we wish we had spent more time with the people we love, and cultivated more meaningful connections at work. It is said, "No one has pictures of their office in their home." When we get home we usually prefer to leave the workday behind. Meanwhile, we display cherished photos of our family in our cubicle, helping us, even while we labor, to take refuge in the elements of our life, chiefly relationships, that give us meaning.

When I was hired to present a corporate seminar on how to maximize employee mental and emotional health, I asked three division managers, "What kinds of things are going on in the lives of your employees outside of work that may be affecting their work?" One manager replied curtly, "That's not our business. People are here to work." Yes, of course, workers' first priority is to do their jobs. Yet more and more businesses are recognizing that the overall well-being of their employees, including their life outside the office, does affect their work. Some corporations are investing millions of dollars to help their employees manage stress because they realize that stressed employees cost the company a lot more in the long run, through accidents, absenteeism, poor performance, pilferage, and insurance premiums. Business, like all of life, is holistic. You cannot slice away one factor of business without considering how that element affects all the other factors. Whenever two people encounter each other, for a moment or a decade, there is a relationship. What we make of that relationship determines all else that follows.

---

### THE MYTH:
Getting the job done is more important
than sustaining healthy relationships.

### THE REALITY:
Healthy relationships are the cornerstone
of a thriving business.

---

## 3. Communication furthers success.

Open, honest, ongoing communication is the vital artery of business. Our interactions suffer more from undercommunication than overcommunication. People make untested assumptions, withhold expression, or deny their observations, which comes back to haunt everyone. My client Tom is a wealthy entrepreneur who sported an apparently ideal marriage and lifestyle. He generated a huge income from his home office on his sprawling estate, where he lived with his wife and two young children. He seemed to have it made. In coaching Tom told me, "I don't understand my wife. She does laundry every day, all day." *Big red flag.* A healthy, happy person does not do laundry every day, all day. I was not surprised when a few months later, Tom informed me that his wife admitted she was having an affair. Soon afterward the couple divorced. If Tom's wife had expressed to her husband her distresses about their marriage, she may not have turned to an affair. The couple may have been able to work out their issues, or they may have parted in a more direct, mature way than one partner going outside the relationship. Communication may not always be pleasant, but, if done consciously, it furthers progress in business and at home.

A colleague told me that she had been married for thirteen years, and then got divorced when "my husband brought his girlfriend home for the weekend." She went on to explain that during all of their marriage she and her husband never fought, "but we also did not communicate."

Never assume that someone else knows your thoughts, feelings, and intentions, or that you know theirs. Although we all have the capacity to be psychic, in most people that faculty has atrophied, so don't expect others to read your mind or assume that you can read theirs. Express yourself when you have something supportive and validating to say, and when you have a statement more difficult. If your intention is sincere, your communication will advance your work. When setting out on a project, check with others to be sure you are on the same page. It's far easier to head off issues or disasters if you do a reality check on your agreements *before* the project begins, or during it, rather than after it.

When we refuse to communicate, we protect our ego and prolong our pain. Subconsciously we know that if we held our hurts, grievances, and upsets up to the light, they would be healed. But we have more of an investment in playing the victim or holding on to our gripes than in resolving them. So we keep our mouth shut and let our pain fester like poison in our gut. Then we wonder why we feel unhappy, get sick, and our relationships and business suffer.

Caroline is the founder and president of a highly respected multinational consulting business. For many years she has worked closely with her dedicated assistant, Joan. One day Joan blew a little issue into a big fight during which she blurted out that Caroline had said something to her many years ago that hurt her deeply. Caroline was shocked; she had no idea any such incident had occurred. "Please tell me what that was," she begged. "I will apologize or we can discuss it, and I can make sure something like that will not happen again."

But still Joan refused to tell Caroline what she was so upset about. Here we have a perfect example of noncommunication as a manipulative tool that backfires and undermines achievement. Joan had more of an investment in holding onto the grievance and being "right" than in resolving the issue. On some level she knew that expressing her experience would lead to righting the perceived wrong, and she was not ready to go there. By contrast, when you speak your truth for the purpose of dissolving interpersonal blocks, that is exactly what will happen. Positive intention creates positive change.

---

## THE MYTH:
Withholding communication keeps you safe.

## THE REALITY:
Honest communication leads to achievement.

---

Sometimes it is necessary to vent your upsets and allow others to vent theirs, before you can come to resolution. I advise my coaches in training to give their clients space to vent before attempting to resolve an issue. You may have to lance a boil and let the pus run out before it can heal. If venting is done in an atmosphere dedicated to healing, it will work. Consciousness training pioneer Werner Erhard conducted an experiment in which he took groups of people who worked together and asked each person to honestly express their feelings about the other members of the group. Erhard found a fascinating pattern: Initially people expressed social niceties. When probed more deeply, they voiced their negative feelings, judgments, and complaints. But, given several more rounds of expression, the comments became more positive. Eventually the workers got to the place where they said, "I appreciate and care about you and I want good for all of us." Some even said, "I love you." Given enough space, anger and upset gave way to kindness, compassion, and creative vision. At our core we all want to feel good about ourselves and each other. Given the opportunity for honest communication, we arrive at that sacred place.

Is it necessary to communicate everything all the time? No, there may be situations where silence is more appropriate. A Buddhist maxim advises, "Speak only when what you have to say is kind, truthful, and helpful." That advice can serve as a powerful ongoing meditation. Ask your inner teacher for guidance on what to say and what not to say, and your communication will rise to maximal productivity.

## 4. We share common ground.

I was riding on an airplane when the captain announced that the chief flight attendant was celebrating her 40th anniversary of flying with this airline. Later I walked to the galley and asked this woman what she had learned in those 40 years. "People are basically the same. We all want the same things for our lives," she answered.

My mentor used to say, "A mystic meets on a point of agreement." We might say the same of a successful leader, salesperson, or administrator. The more we focus on our differences, the more we widen the illusory gap between people and distance ourselves from our goals. The more we join together, the more we erase that gap.

---

### THE MYTH:
Divisiveness yields victory.

### THE REALITY:
Real strength comes from joining.

---

We can even use parting as an opportunity to join. Longfellow said, "Great is the art of beginning. Even greater is the art of ending." Because we are always in relationship with our co-workers, how we complete our business together is as important as how we initiate or conduct it. Over many years as a business owner I have had to fire some employees. While the process is never fun, in most cases I have been successful to create a win-win result because I respect and honor the employee even through the termination process.

My assistant Megan was continually distracted by taking personal mobile phone calls during work hours. Overhearing some of the conversations, I gleaned that she was organizing community events and concerts. After I asked Megan to put aside her phone during work hours and she continued to use it, I could not justify keeping her in the position. I told her, "I know that you are passionate about your community organizing, and I respect you for it. But you are so involved with these projects that your work in this office is suffering seriously. So I am going to let you go so you can pursue your passion. That will also free me to get someone for this position who wants to be here and is fully present with the job." Megan understood and we had an amicable parting.

Megan went on to establish a successful business as an event planner, and I filled her role with someone who did a far better job. Several years later when I presented a program in Megan's town, she was one of the first to show up. "I had to get my Alan fix," she told me as she entered. Her presence warmed my heart, as it indicated that our relationship remained not only intact, but mutually supportive.

Of course it is not always possible to end a working relationship in such a friendly manner. But it may be possible a lot more than you expect. Even if the connection does not end on a positive note, your role remains the same: Speak your truth, respect the other person as well as yourself, and trust that the changes you initiate will be in the best interest of everyone involved.

---

### THE MYTH:

Ending a business relationship has to be acrimonious.

### THE REALITY:

It is possible to part harmoniously.

---

## 5. Integrity works.

When I was shopping my first book to distributors, a small but growing specialty-subject company wooed me. At the time, the company represented a number of authors who have since become quite well known. When word got around that I had signed with this company, I received a mysterious phone call from one of its former clients. "The owner is a crook," he told me. "Don't work with him." I wrote off this fellow's warning as that of a disgruntled customer and went ahead anyway.

The company sold lots of books on my behalf, and I was pleased. A year later I received a phone call from the owner's executive assistant, whom I had gotten to know through our interchanges. "I need to speak to you in person," she told me. We made a lunch date and this woman drove two hours to my town. There she told me, "The company has been selling a lot more of your books than the owner is paying you for. I see the sales income and I see the checks he is sending you. He is shorting you big-time. I will be quitting soon because I cannot work in a business absent of integrity. I wanted you to know this before I leave." I trusted this woman's advice, and I pulled the plug on distributing through this company. Eventually the other authors learned of the same issue one way or another, and they all quit.

Ironically, some of those authors became some of the most successful in the industry. You would recognize their names if I mentioned them. One established a hugely successful multimillion-dollar-income publishing company. While the owner without integrity pocketed some cash by cheating his authors, if he had paid them fairly and they stayed with him, he would have earned many millions of dollars over time. By contrast, after I left his company I went to Hay House, established by Louise Hay. Soon afterward I received a letter that Louise sent to all of her authors, thanking them for their service and telling them, "I love to send out royalty checks." How many business leaders affirm that they love to pay their employees well? Hay House has been very good to me over many years. The company has high integrity and seeks to make its employees and customers happy.

While integrity may appear to cost you more in the short run, it will gain you huge returns in the long run.

## 6. Boundaries empower everyone.

To achieve maximal success, you must say no to activities or policies that distract you from your goals. Many people feel guilty about setting boundaries. Yet healthy boundaries help people on both sides of the fence.

The CEO of a company built by a successful author and teacher told me that when the company was first established, he hired people who were fans of the author (i.e., groupies). The employees wanted to work in a "spiritual" atmosphere and have contact with their revered mentor. The problem, the CEO explained, was that the workers were not particularly qualified and their emotionalism distracted them from doing their work. "I would pass a worker's desk and find her crying because she was processing her breakup. Others came in late because they needed to complete their argument with their husband before they could go to work. One fellow could not focus because he was having an out-of-body experience. The office became a self-help seminar and jobs were not getting done." From that point on, the CEO hired only people who were not enamored with the teacher or even familiar with him. Instead he hired only people who were qualified for the position. After that crucial decision, the company stabilized and went on to do very well.

A wisely stated no to what you don't want makes way for a strong yes to what you do want. People who don't match your company's values or practices belong elsewhere. Call people to integrity by asking them to do what they are here to do and to refrain from nonproductive behaviors. Trust your well-considered boundaries. They will help everyone involved.

---

### THE MYTH:

Saying no is cruel and is a cause for guilt.

### THE REALITY:

A wisely chosen no supports everyone.

---

Now let's look at where you stand with your boundary setting, and how you can empower yourself, others, and your work by setting boundaries that work.

## SETTING HEALTHY BOUNDARIES

*A boundary I have had a hard time setting and I need to set:*

_____

_____

_____

*How this boundary can help me:*

_____

_____

_____

*How this boundary can help the others involved:*

_____

_____

_____

*A step I will take to set this boundary:*

_____

_____

_____

Repeat this process for several different boundaries that can help you and others.

## 7. Let joy be your compass.

Legendary mythologist Joseph Campbell coined the phrase "follow your bliss." This maxim applies just as much in the business world as it does during your "free time." All time is free time because we are always free to choose the thoughts, attitudes, and feelings that determine our experience.

Try all invitations, options, and choices on for size. Be honest about whether the path you are considering lights you or dims you. Are you excited and inspired about what is before you, or is it just another obligation dictated by fear, guilt, or tradition? Build your skill to follow your bliss by practicing on the little decisions of the day. What would you like to eat for lunch? Which project speaks to you most strongly? Who would you most like to work with? Do you really care to participate in that gossip session? Do you need to Skype with the East Coast office, or would a phone call do? If one option offers even a teeny bit more aliveness than another, choose that path. After a while you will develop a keen relationship with the voice of joy. When you let it guide you in little decisions, you will gain the capacity to hear and act on it for more crucial decisions.

In some instances, you may be required to do things you do not find attractive or exciting. In that case, reframe the situation so you find a perspective that feels more peaceful. No one likes to go to a funeral, but if you consider that this is your way of honoring the person who has passed on and supporting their family, your sense of purpose is edified and you find a ray of soul satisfaction even while a part of you resists. Walking into a meeting about a problematic situation may feel like a downer, but when you consider that this is a step toward getting the situation handled, you gain strength in purpose. It's unpleasant to have to drop a project that has not succeeded, but when you envision that you will replace that project with a new and better one, there is light at the end of the tunnel. Even tunnels can be fun. People pay money at amusement parks to go on rides through tunnels and come out on the other side. The contrast between the darkness of the tunnel and emerging into the light can be exhilarating.

Allow your spirit to be a primary decision maker rather than just your head. You cannot and will not think your way through life. The intellect is but one tool in your kit. The heart, or internal guide, is a powerful tool too often underused in business. The most successful business people stay on track with what lights them. When you trust your aliveness more than your numbness, you will join their ranks.

## THE MYTH:

Fulfilling burdensome obligations paves the path to success.

## THE REALITY:

Following the path lit by joy takes you to
valuable places that guilt cannot reach.

## 8. Develop and trust your discernment.

Many people will tell you how you should conduct your business and your life. Some advice may be helpful to you, and some may not apply to you at all. Your pathway to success is unique to your talents, visions, and purpose. Try all advice on for size, and be impeccably honest about what matches you. People who tell you what to do may mean well, but they are proceeding from their own values, which may or may not match yours. You are the one who must live with the results of your decisions, so be sure your decisions proceed from your inner choices, not external influence.

When our stove's control panel ceased to function, I phoned a well-known national appliance service to request a repair. When I told the agent what was happening, her voice grew ominous. "You have a serious problem, sir. Your heating element has gone bad and you will need a new control panel, both of which are very expensive. You may need to replace your stove entirely. But I have good news. We have an annual service plan that will lower your cost, and . . ." blah, blah, blah. The service plan was expensive, and I would still have to pay for part of the repairs. After listening for a while I realized that the agent was not at all qualified to diagnose the issue; she was simply trained to sell me a service plan. When I told her I was not interested, she intensified her sales pitch. Finally, I politely hung up. I then found a local repairman, a heckuva nice guy who came out the next day and quickly and easily replaced the control board at a fraction of the national company's estimated repair cost or its service plan. Thinking back on the agent's sales pitch, the more I listened, the more I felt like I was being sucked into quicksand. When I connected with the local repairman, I felt liberated. In each case my gut was guiding me. That's how inner direction works.

You will encounter many options on the smorgasbord of business and life. You are working your way along a long buffet table with hundreds of dishes to choose from. Not every item matches your taste, and you cannot choose them all. Just as you would carefully select the items you desire on a buffet, carefully choose from the options offered you in business. Certain ones belong to you and others do not. Be confident to take what is appropriate for you and leave what is not. Make sure you are eating your own lunch and not someone else's. We can all enjoy a satisfying lunch with different items on our plates.

## 9. Take the high road.

When you encounter people or situations operating at a low frequency characterized by anger, fear, jealousy, competitiveness, or lethargy, don't go there with them. Instead, remain established in the higher frequency of joy, positive vision, and creativity. Much of the world's activity is motivated by insanity. Your task is to remain sane even if those around you act crazy. One of the questions I am most frequently asked is, "I work in an office where people are very negative. They gossip, criticize, and argue. How can I enjoy my day and do my job well anyway?" I give such clients several prescriptions:

- Before you go to work, take some time to establish your vision for how you would like to feel and act throughout your day. Sit quietly and produce a mental movie of your ideal scenario. In your mind, play out how well your work-day can go, until the experience feels real.

- Mentally surround yourself with a field of white light. Declare that only energies and activities that match your best interests can enter your field, and darker, more negative energies cannot affect you. You may be aware of undesirable actions from a distance, but they will not penetrate your domain. During your day, renew your intentional field whenever you need to.

- Define the purpose of your day as to stay at peace. Your goal shifts from "How much work can I get done?" to "How happy can I stay?" No matter what anyone says or what events transpire, maintain your chosen attitude. If you remain at peace at the end of the day, your day is a success.

- When someone else goes low, you go high. Don't fall into the same delusion that has caused the other person to act cruelly. People connected to their spiritual Source are always more effective than those who are discon-nected. When darkness and light meet, light establishes reality.

- Regard people who challenge you as angels sent to help you build spiritual mastery. They force you to dig into yourself, identify your true values, and live from them. Such people have not come to deter you, but to advance you.

One of my clients was annoyed by her overbearing boss, and she was thinking about quitting. I suggested that before she went to work each day, she sit quietly for a few minutes and surround the fellow in light. See the best in him, regard him as a little boy calling for love, and mentally enfold him in appreciation and blessing. She practiced this vision, and the next time I saw her she told me, "My boss was transferred."

All relationships are based on matching energy. Like pieces of Velcro that stick together because two sets of hooks interlock, relationships stick together because both parties agree on the nature of the interaction. When one person withdraws from the agreement and ceases to engage in negativity, that relationship must change. If a co-worker wants to dwell in upset and you refuse to do so, that person will have to meet you on higher ground or go elsewhere. Even if that person refuses to change, you will not be affected by him. You may hardly even be aware of him. Imagine going to a multiplex movie theater where different movies are playing simultaneously. You are sitting in a theater where a lighthearted comedy or inspirational story is playing. On the other side of the theater wall, a violent drama or noisy action film is showing. You remain involved in your chosen experience while those watching the other movie are involved in their experience. You might occasionally hear a distant boom or a character yelling in the neighboring theater's movie, but you are so immersed in your movie that you hardly notice it and it doesn't affect you in the least. You have established your attention in your preferred reality. What other people choose for themselves is less important than what you choose for yourself. I have heard many stories of relationships and situations miraculously changing when one person elevates their attitude.

## THE MYTH:

You can defeat negative people by battling them on the field they establish.

## THE REALITY:

When you rise above negativity, you are in the strongest position to overcome it.

Now let's take a situation that is challenging you and shift it by establishing yourself at a higher level:

## TAKE THE HIGH ROAD

*A situation in which someone close to me is immersed in negative energy:*

_____

_____

_____

*How I respond by slipping into negativity:*

_____

_____

_____

*The result of me stepping into darkness:*

_____

_____

_____

*How I would be thinking, feeling, and acting if I chose to stay in the light:*

_____

_____

_____

*The benefits that could accrue to me as I take the high road:*

_____

_____

_____

*The benefits that could accrue to the other person(s) as I take the high road:*

_____

_____

_____

*An action step I will take that demonstrates I am choosing the high road:*

_____

_____

## 10. There is no death–only transformation.

Nothing in form lasts forever. This principle applies to business relationships, projects, jobs, careers, companies, and living situations. While we may enjoy a sense of security to believe that what is will always be, the truth is that what is will one day give way to something else. The only constant in the manifested universe is change.

What appears to die is transformed and reborn as something else. If a job or company dies, it's not the end of the world. It's just the end of a phase. A new form awaits. Death and birth go together like two sides of a coin. What is born dies, and something greater comes alive. If you have a business relationship or job that lasts for a long time, bless and enjoy it. When it comes to an end, don't lament or resist. If it had a further purpose, it would continue. The universe is economical in not wasting life force on what no longer serves. It will brilliantly invest life force in something better. The only situation worse than a business phase ending would be for it to continue after it has lived out its usefulness. Some musicians, artists, and writers simply rehash the same material in a thousand different forms. Truly creative people, on the other hand, are eager to stretch, be challenged, and dive into new and varied expressions. Actors Meryl Streep, Dustin Hoffman, and Tom Hanks consistently choose unconventional versatile roles. If the Beatles had stayed with "Yeah, yeah, yeah" for their entire careers, the world would have missed the sophisticated compositions their music grew into as they matured. Hiding in the known becomes deadening; launching into the unknown is life giving. You cannot cling to the old and embrace the new. An ending marks a milestone of transition to better. Reach for what that better could be, and you will bless the current ending as a gift.

---

## THE MYTH:
When something good ends, there is loss.

## THE REALITY:
When something good ends, something new is created.

---

There is no such thing as business, as Robert Holden stated, because there is only life. Business represents one quadrant of life but is not separate from it. Question, challenge, and move beyond any business belief or practice that opposes or excuses itself from the universal laws established to bring us joy, well-being, and success. We do not have the right or power to bend these laws. If we recognized the state of grace in which we live, we would not want to alter truth in the slightest. Universal principles form the underpinning of all that is good. You cannot set business, money, relationships, politics, science, education, health care, or any other human affair in a room by itself and expect it to work. Everything in life is connected to everything else. If you attempt to disconnect business from all that lives, you deny its power to bless you. To fully succeed in your career, let the life that is business live through you.

**TRUTH #9**
**WHAT MAKES LIFE WORK MAKES BUSINESS WORK**

# ILLUSION #10:
# YOU MUST SACRIFICE YOUR LIFE FOR WORK

In the Andes Mountains two native tribes were constantly feuding with each other. One tribe lived in the lowlands and the other high in the mountains. One night the highlanders raided the lowlanders' village and kidnapped a baby. The next morning a group of men from the lowlanders' village organized a search party to scale the mountain and retrieve the child. But the tribesmen, unskilled at climbing, were hard-pressed to ascend. The steep slope, thick jungle, and unfamiliar territory were daunting, and after several hours the party decided to abandon their mission and turn back.

Just then they noticed a woman descending from above them on the mountain. As she drew closer, they were astonished to see it was the mother of the kidnapped baby, holding the child in her arms.

When the woman reached the search party, the leader asked her, "How did you make your way to the top of the mountain and retrieve your child when we could not even complete the climb?"

"It's not your baby," she answered.

When your motivation and intention are strong, you do what you need to do because no other option is acceptable. Your life is your baby, and your work has stolen it. Fear and illusion have usurped the throne of your kingdom. How badly do you want your life back?

Many people have a hard time separating their job from their personal life. Work becomes a consuming addiction. They take projects home, they labor over emails and spreadsheets late into the night, they are available at all hours for texts and phone calls, they sacrifice weekends and holidays, and their family life suffers. Frustration, irritability, and depression arise, accompanied by health-related issues. Spouses pressure wage earners to take more time off and be with the kids, with disappointing results. After a certain point your work owns you; the habit becomes a tyrant. You are overwhelmed with a deluge of work and have little, if any, time for play or renewal. This is the dilemma that many of us face.

Yet, like the mother who retrieved her baby because her intention was uncompromising, if you sincerely desire a life besides work, it will be yours. While it appears that other people or conditions are forcing you to do things you do not prefer, it is not so. Everything you do represents your choice. As long as you believe you don't have a choice, you will not recognize or exercise your inherent power. The moment you accept 100 percent responsibility for your past experience, you gain 100 percent of the power to create future experiences you prefer.

## LET GO AND THRIVE

In Japan, overwork is one of the most serious problems confronting the culture. So many people literally work themselves to death that the Japanese have a word for it: *karoshi*. Japan also has one of the highest suicide rates in the world. While many of us do not work ourselves to physical death, we become so enmeshed in our careers that we commit emotional or psychological suicide. We trudge through our days and get things done, but we feel numb, bored, and empty, and our long to-do list remains undone. In recent years, zombie and vampire movies have become quite popular. The subject matter of our cultural entertainment represents internal dynamics projected outward. Many people have become spiritual zombies and others have become so depleted of life force that they have to suck it from others. A large sector of our population is composed of the living dead. Just because we walk and breathe does not mean we live. Real life is defined by the presence and expression of joy.

You were not born to work yourself to depression, illness, or death. You are a living spirit, created in the image and likeness of God, here to radiate light and aliveness to the world and enjoy all the benefits of your divine heritage. Any other experience does not befit you or your mission. If you have slipped away from your purpose, it's time to come home.

Lester Levenson was a physicist who worked himself into multiple health issues, including a serious heart condition. At the age of 42, he was told by his doctor that his heart was so fragile he would be dead within three months; he could drop at any moment. That prognosis got Lester's attention. He went home and thought about the issues in his life that were stressing him, and he decided to find a way to let them go. Levenson took each troubling matter and methodically released it, relieving himself of his sense of burden. The more he let go, the better he felt. He said, "In the process of . . . unloading all the subconscious concepts and pressures. . . I discovered I was getting happier, freer, lighter, and feeling better in general." As Levenson's attitude and health continued to improve, he passed his method along to others. Because he discovered his release technique in Sedona, Arizona, he called it "The Sedona Method" and taught it to many thousands of people. Levenson lived 43 happy years beyond his diagnosis, and to this day he shines as a model of the simple yet life-changing power of release.

---

## THE MYTH:
To succeed more, you must work more.

## THE REALITY:
To succeed more, renew yourself more.

---

## BELIEFS RUN THE SHOW

If you want to achieve a more rewarding work/life balance, discover and heal the beliefs that are causing the imbalance. You can't just say, "I need to set better boundaries." Setting better boundaries will help, but *why* you set them is the key to making them work. When you pierce to the causational level of an issue, you can ameliorate or remove the need to struggle with boundary setting. People who seek to lose weight know, "I should have a better diet," but it is only when overeaters understand *why* they are overeating that they go on to improve their diet and weight. Anxious eating is one of the principal causes of excess weight. When an individual identifies, faces, and overcomes the anxiety, the desire for comfort food and the poundage it brings dissolves. Here let's remember Thoreau's observation, "There are a thousand hacking at the branches of evil to one who is striking at the root."

What would someone have to believe in order to create a life in which toil suffocates joy? There are several possibilities: (1) You believe you must earn your good by struggle, suffering, and sacrifice. If you don't bust your butt and display the appropriate battle scars, you are a slacker; (2) You value the payoffs of a top-heavy job, such as money, power, and prestige more than activities that feed your soul; (3) You feel guilty or are afraid to say no to your boss or turn down projects; (4) You seek to prove yourself to your family, friends, religion, society, or dead relatives; and (5) Constantly working distracts you from the pain and issues of your life that you would rather not confront.

The first step to healing this imbalance is to recognize the shallow or illusory rewards the external behavior is bringing you. They are not real rewards at all, but addictions that distance you from the inner peace you yearn for. Here are some insights to offset the illusions causing overwork I noted above: (1) Spending many hours a day to prove you are not a slacker is a self-punishing pattern in which you trade the treasure of aliveness for the puniest of pellets. (2) Getting money and power instead of the joy of family, friends, and the vitality of your spirit nets you the grand booby prize. (3) When you live and act to escape guilt, you deny your inherent worth and innocence. (4) When you seek achievement to prove yourself to others, you have bestowed them with undue power over your happiness. (5) The pain and issues you seek to avoid by overworking are really arrows pointing you to where true healing, awakening, and transformation result when you face those issues and heal them.

*A Course in Miracles* calls us to evaluate every potential action by asking ourselves, "What is this for?" Or, "Why am I doing this?" If your answer is connected to deep fulfillment, you are on the right track. If you are engaging for reasons that drag you away from inner peace, they are worthless. Be fearlessly honest about your motivation and the beliefs that are fueling your action, and you will find your way out of the forest and into the light.

---

## THE MYTH:

You improve your life by altering your behavior.

## THE REALITY:

You improve your life by discovering the beliefs that motivate your actions and replacing self-sabotaging beliefs with beliefs that fulfill you.

---

The self-introspection exercise below will help you shine light on beliefs you are holding that serve you and those that work against your happiness. Honesty is your best friend as you peel away self-defeating notions to reveal the empowering truth.

## ▪ ▪ ▪ BOGUS BELIEF BUSTERS ▪ ▪ ▪

*Oppressive beliefs I hold that cause me to overwork:*

_____

_____

_____

*Actions I take based on those beliefs:*

_____

_____

_____

*Painful results of those actions in my body, emotions, relation-ships, and business:*

_____

_____

_____

*Healthier beliefs I could substitute for the oppressive beliefs:*

_____

_____

_____

*What I would be doing differently if I proceeded from healthier beliefs:*

_____

_____

_____

*Positive results that would accrue to me as a result of me upgrading my beliefs and actions:*

_____

_____

_____

*Positive results that would accrue to others as a result of me upgrading my beliefs and actions:*

_____

_____

_____

## SIGNS YOU HAVE CROSSED THE LINE

The compassionate universe is eager and willing to give you signals of guidance on your journey to achieve a more rewarding work/life balance. When you begin to work too much, your body and/or emotions will give you clear indications that you have crossed a critical line. You may get a tickle in your throat, headache, back pain, indigestion, or a skin eruption. Or you may become irritable, fatigued, get into arguments, or have accidents. You know what your personal symptoms are. When such signs show up, the universe is letting you know that it's time to stop, step back, lighten up, rest, and renew. Make up your mind that the next time such signs appear, you will heed them.

If you have missed the signs in the past or not acted on them, don't worry—you will have more chances. The universe cares so much about your well-being that it will not let you keep heading in a direction that will hurt you. Pay attention to what's working and what's not working for you, and be honest about what brings you life and what deadens you. When you do your part, the universe will help with the details.

Some highways are embedded with "rumble strips," up-raised bumps along the side of the road to alert drivers who fall asleep and start to veer off the highway. They make a loud "bum-pety-bumpety" noise when the car hits them, and jar the driver to wake up and get back on course. Likewise, your symptoms of stress are trying to get your attention to back off, slow down, and redirect. If you heed them, your course correction will restore your health and foster your success. If you ignore them, work harder to bury them, or distract yourself with some self-numbing behavior like drinking, anxious eating, or compulsive shopping, your issues will exacerbate. Like an alarm clock that starts with a soft tone that grows louder the longer you sleep, your signals will increase in volume until they get your attention. Such "in-your-face" events are not a punishment. They are wake-up calls. If you listen to your guidance, you can make decisions seamlessly and painlessly. Life brilliantly and compassionately reminds you when you are not loving yourself and guides you back to well-being.

---

## THE MYTH:

You can ignore or override the signals the universe is sending you to stay on track with your health and success.

## THE REALITY:

When you act on guidance through signs coming to you, you find the shortest and easiest path to well-being and prosperity.

---

Now let's make good use of the important signs you are receiving that show you that you are overworking, and then identify healthy replacements for self-defeating behavior.

## ■ ■ ■ ACT ON THE MESSAGE ■ ■ ■

*Physical, emotional, or mental signs that tell me I have crossed a line and I am working too much:*

_____

_____

_____

*How I typically respond (for example, work harder, take a pill, watch TV):*

_____

_____

_____

*Healthier alternatives I could choose (for example, take a walk, have a nap, do yoga):*

_____

_____

_____

*What I will do the next time I get a sign I am overworking:*

_____

_____

_____

■ ■ ■

## FROM BALANCE TO BLEND

Work/life balance is a hot topic because nearly everyone needs it and hardly anyone has fully achieved it. Yet how we think about something makes all the difference in whether or not it works for us. If you think of work and life as two separate experiences, polarized with a gap between them, and you must struggle to balance them like a tightrope walker who may fall and be killed if he slips, you will not succeed. You will never find peace trying to harmonize distinct and opposing forces. If you shift your goal to create a work/life *blend,* you are one step closer to making them both work on your behalf.

Work and life are not enemies. They are branches that spring from the same tree of life. Both are expressions of your passion, vision, talent, prosperity, and unique gifts. If you pit them against each other and think, "one at the expense of the other," you will have neither. If, instead, you merge them by finding how they can work together and complement each other, valuing both without one canceling the other, you have taken your second important step. Here are the key ways to create that life-giving blend:

### 1. Be honest about the pain or difficulty your sense of imbalance is causing.

I asked a Buddhist teacher, "If you do not know that you are suffering, are you still suffering?" He answered, "That is the worst kind of suffering." Do not accept suffering as your lot on the job or in life, or attempt to distract yourself or gloss over it. Reframe work/life imbalance as a call to tell more truth about where you are and where you want to be. *A Course in Miracles* asks us, "Who would attempt to fly with the tiny wings of a sparrow when the mighty power of an eagle has been given him?" Honesty about your experience is the first act toward gaining your greater wings.

### 2. Examine your motivation.

How much of your work proceeds from joy and creativity, and how much from fear or lack? There is no cosmic decree about how much a person should work. If you are passionate about your endeavor, 12 hours a day is not too much. If you are laboring under guilt, rote, obligation, or boredom, two hours is too much. There *is* a cosmic law about the relationship between motivation and success. What proceeds from aliveness flourishes. What proceeds from numbness is doomed.

In the engaging biography *Elon Musk*, author Ashlee Vance recounts the demanding but exhilarating years when Musk's then-fledgling company SpaceX was striving to break into the space exploration market. Musk chose the remote Kwajalein Atoll in the South Pacific as the company's rocket test launch site. There he stationed a team of dedicated engineers who worked day and night to get the rockets and the business off the ground. The team labored 16 hours every day under grueling conditions in an extremely isolated location with few creature comforts and minimal supplies. One engineer recounts, "Every . . . person on that island was a . . . star . . . they were always holding seminars on radios or the engine. It was such an invigorating place." While the surface conditions of these engineers' jobs were torturous, the workers were spiritually exhilarated.

British anthropologist Jane Goodall is respected worldwide as a champion of primates and the environment. At age 83 (as of this writing), Ms. Goodall's passion for her mission continues to mobilize superhuman energy. She constantly jaunts around the globe delivering lectures and gathering donations to help apes and the planet survive. At a time of life when many other people have retired, withdrawn, or died, this woman is so enthusiastic about her project that she has access to boundless power and resources, which contribute to her good health and fortitude.

Orchestra leader André Rieu, whom I mentioned earlier, is another world-change agent who defies the "laws" of overwork. At age 69, Rieu treks about the globe with his 120-member orchestra and staff, traveling or delivering high-energy concerts nearly half the nights of every year, spanning many continents. Rieu is confident in his philosophy: "I've changed my life to make sure I work only on what I love . . . Everything is about the power of the mind. Your health is in your head. When you are satisfied with your work, you don't get ill."

To an untrained observer, these dedicated creators appear to be imbalanced with heavy, almost impossible work schedules. But to them, a labor of love is no labor at all.

By contrast, some people work seven hours a day in an air-conditioned office with state-of-the-art equipment but hate every hour and come home exhausted. Others are counting the days until they can retire from the military at age 37. Others go through the motions of their profession, but their minds and hearts are elsewhere. People who soar and those who struggle all demonstrate that attitude creates experience and motivation determines success.

Other people minimize their work time and achieve remarkable results. Marc Allen is the co-founder and president of New World Library, a self-help publisher that has scored some mega-successful books, including Eckhart Tolle's *The Power of Now*, Deepak Chopra's *The Seven Spiritual Laws of Success,* and Shakti Gawain's *Creative Visualization*. These bestsellers, along with other popular titles, have netted Allen and his company many millions of dollars. Yet Allen is as far from being a workaholic as any successful person could be. He has chosen what he calls "the path of laziness" and dubs himself a "Type Z" personality. He sleeps until 11 A.M., hangs out in his hot tub, gets into the office around 1 P.M., and doesn't work on Mondays. This lifestyle works for Allen as well as 16-hour workdays work for Elon Musk's team, because both are acting in harmony with their beliefs about how to get things done. There is no one way to get things done. Things get done when the life you live expresses who you are.

If you feel energized and creative, no matter how much time you work, you have found your right livelihood. If you feel burdened or burnt out, you have veered. Do whatever you need to do to bring your activities into alignment with your values.

## ▪ ▪ ▪ GETTING ALIGNED ▪ ▪ ▪

Work activities that energize me:

_____

_____

Work activities that deplete me:

_____

_____

A step I could take to increase or maximize the activities that energize me:

_____

_____

A step I could take to decrease or eliminate the activities that deplete me:

_____

_____

How great it would feel to do more of what I love and less of what I detest:

_____

_____

How my career, health, relationships, and life could change as I do what brings me joy:

_____

_____

▪ ▪ ▪

### 3. Express your desire for a healthier blend.

Reach out to someone you trust and express your desire for change. There is no shame in admitting that you are working too hard; to the contrary, such a statement is a mark of integrity. Speak to your spouse, a friend, mentor, minister, counselor, or coach. Those who care about you will support you.

A number of years ago I realized I was spending too much time and energy on my work and not enough with my partner and family. I told Dee, who was delighted to hear that I wanted to achieve that shift. I went out for a few hours and when I returned I found our living room brimming with balloons, accompanied by a recording of Kenny Loggins singing, "Come celebrate me home." I was deeply touched by Dee's show of support that helped me create a course correction I have largely maintained since that time.

### 4. Amp up the activities that reward you more than work.

There are things you love to do that nourish your soul more than working. Perhaps you like to walk in nature, travel, play music, journal, meditate, go to the theater, get together with valued friends, have dinner at your favorite restaurant, or attend uplifting seminars. When you engage in activities that feed your spirit, the contrast between how you feel when you do them and how you feel when you work is staggering. The more you participate in what lifts you, the more that feeling will become your prevalent experience.

We have some neighbors who purchased a parcel of land near us and have been building their house and cultivating their garden. Dee and I drove by their place to say hello and see how they were doing. We found the couple clearing some brush. They looked exhilarated. As they spoke about the immense joy they were receiving from immersing themselves in their passionate project, the husband told us that he used to sit at the computer all day with work-related tasks. Now he is enjoying his house project so much that he is outdoors all day and he waits until the evening to answer his emails. "My clients used to expect an answer from me within ten minutes," he said. "Now they know that twenty-four hours is my time frame for a response." Although this couple is in their 50s, they looked like a couple of teenagers.

You can't get rid of a negative behavior by fighting it or trying to squelch it. You have to replace it with something more desirable. If your child picks up a dangerous object to play with and you take it away, the child may go into a fit. If you replace the item with a safe toy, you have eliminated the danger and the child is happy. The ego is an immature part of our mind that is fascinated with dangerous toys. Give your mind something more productive to attend to and you replace overwork with soul satisfaction. My teacher used to talk about "jamming the signal" of a radio station, a technique used in war. Two different radio stations cannot occupy the same frequency. One or the other will prevail. Fill your mind and life with activities that fulfill you, and unsatisfying activities will have to vacate the premises.

## 5. Set healthy boundaries and stick with them.

Decide how much you will work, and be true to your plan. Make an agreement with your partner (or yourself) that you will leave the office at 5 P.M., and then keep your agreement. I know a couple who work at home. They told me, "The computers go off at six o'clock. Then we have dinner and go into the living room to read, snuggle, or watch a movie." If you make an agreement with your partner, hold each other accountable. Gently or humorously remind each other when one or both of you have gone beyond your boundaries.

One year I decided to take a sabbatical. Several months went by and I was still working. I couldn't turn off the habit. Then I had a coaching session with my mentor. I told her, "I am working too much." Although she knew I had committed to taking time off, she playfully asked me, "Have you thought about taking a sabbatical?" Her question reminded me that I had not been true to my promise to myself. From that moment on I quit working and I reaped the rewards of time off for the remainder of that period.

The New Testament tells us, "Let your 'yes' be a 'yes' and your 'no' be a 'no.' All else is the work of the devil." The devil, in this case, is muddy thinking and weak decision-making. The secret to saying a firm no to overworking or any other undesirable activity is to remember the yes that the no is making way for. Saying no to working on weekends is saying yes to quality time with your kids. Saying no to an invitation to a boring gathering is saying yes to giving yourself time to develop your passionate project. Saying no to dating someone you are not attracted to is saying yes to being available to someone you find more attractive. A real no is the doorway to a real yes.

### 6. Build self-nurturing activities into your schedule.

If you wait until you have a chance to do something fun, it will keep being delayed or not happen at all. The work habit has a way of crowding your schedule and keeping you stuck in your office or routine. Every activity has momentum and generates more of itself. Don't wait for work to release you. Release yourself. Set a time in advance when you will get a massage, take a yoga class, visit a relative, get a coaching session, go to the beach, attend an art exhibit, or take a vacation. You will be glad you did as you recognize that self-renewal is not a matter of chance, but choice.

### 7. Apply spiritual economics.

While you may be careful about how you invest your money, you may not be as careful about how you invest your time and energy. Are your hours at work yielding more joy, or more stress? If struggle is a theme, it's time to revisit your investment strategy.

We are told, "Time is money." But time is a far more valuable commodity than money. Actor David Cassidy uttered four final words on his deathbed: "So much wasted time." David's daughter Katie, who was at her father's side, declared, "This will be a daily reminder for me to share my gratitude with those I love and to never waste another minute."

In biblical times, farmers gave their land a Sabbath. Every seventh year they refrained from planting a crop so the land could renew itself. The farmers also took that year to fertilize the soil. While the farmers did not accrue the benefit of the crops they might have harvested during that year, the field yielded more and better over the six years that followed. So it is with work and rest. While it appears that working continuously will give you the highest benefit, taking a rest will serve you more in the long run.

Consider taking some kind of sabbatical for yourself. Designate one day a week when you will not work; perhaps even put your phone aside. You may be amazed to discover that not only will you survive a day away from work, but you will gain so much clarity and energy that when you return you will be far happier and more productive. Or take one weekend a month. Or several weeks or even months out of a year. Take mini-sabbaticals each day as well. Step back for 15 minutes here and there and renew yourself by sitting in the sun, walking in the park, doing some yoga, listening to your favorite music, or taking a nap. When you make self-renewal a top priority, you will feel better and your work will become more productive.

## 8. Recognize the benefit your self-renewal brings to others.

When you are happy and vibrant, you uplift others and you are a blessing to the world. When you are irritable, burnt out, or emotionally absent, you are sucking life force from your workplace. You contribute as much through your state of being as through your product or service. Don't be seduced by form at the expense of spirit. Your business is a vehicle to deliver your spirit to a world hungry for upliftment. We are told in the Bible, "You are the light of the world. Don't hide your light under a bushel." If you really want to help the world, do whatever it takes to make and keep yourself happy. Rest, renew, and recharge not just for your own sake, but for everyone you touch.

## 9. Revisit your choice of work.

If your work is dragging you down more than lifting you, it may be time to reconsider if you are in your right place. Many people take jobs for reasons that do not serve them. They accept the first position offered; take a job for the money only; yield to pressure from their parents, spouse, peers, or religion; continue to do what they have always done just because the territory is familiar; choose a job for a convenient location; have unrealistic fantasies about where the job will lead them; stay in the job because they would feel guilty for leaving; or other reasons that miss the bull's-eye of pure intention. If you hate your job or you feel worse at the end of your workday, you cannot afford to continue.

Consider what a more passion-based career would look and feel like for you. When exploring possibilities, use your intuition and imagination rather than your reasoning mind alone. The intellect has a way of slicing, dicing, dissecting, and suffocating good ideas before they get birthed. You can put your ideas to the rational test later. For now, let your vision soar. Thinking out of the box is the first step to getting out of the box. Ask yourself, "If time, money, experience, and approval from others were not factors, what would I like to do?" In that introspection free of constriction, you may come up with bold and stimulating ideas. Upon further exploration, you may realize that your vision may not be just a wild fantasy. It may be doable, and you can take at least a small step in that direction, which leads to subsequent steps and eventual manifestation.

## 10. Find a way to bring more life to your work.

While it may be tempting to quit your job, and in some situations that is what you need to do, in many cases it is more profitable to upgrade your job from within it. Instead of seeking life elsewhere, bring more life to where you stand. There are two ways to do this.

The first is to re-create or renegotiate your position so it becomes more of a match to your vision, talents, and passion. If you are an entrepreneur, you have vast control over your work life. Be more honest about what you want to do and what you don't want to do. Amp up the desirable aspects and delegate or eliminate the undesirable ones. "If it's not fun, hire it done." There are people who would love to do what you hate to do. Let them do what they do best so you can free yourself to do what you do best.

You may be able to take a boring or rote situation and upgrade it so it is more fun. I saw a documentary about a dentist who was an avid *Star Trek* fan. He redecorated his office to resemble the bridge of the Starship Enterprise. He and his office staff wore *Star Trek* crew uniforms and had the show's paraphernalia around the office. Suddenly, going to work became fun for the dentist, and his clients got a kick out of a more relaxed and playful atmosphere than they had ever experienced at a dentist's office. That fellow masterfully demonstrated the motto, "Take what you have and make what you want."

If you work for a company or other employer, you have less latitude in ways to re-create your job. But you can speak to your employer and look for ways to renegotiate what you are doing. Don't just complain about what is not working. Show up with a positive vision of what you would like to do instead, and how that activity could benefit the company. Bring your passion to the discussion. As an entrepreneur who has had many employees, I want my staff to feel happy and excited about their jobs. I make every effort to help them keep their soul alive in their work. I recognize the vital correlation between job satisfaction and productivity. If your employer wants you to excel in your position, he or she will be open to considering options that could work for both of you.

The second way to bring more life to your job applies in situations in which you have little or no latitude in your duties. Perhaps your role is fixed and the job simply is what it is. In that case, here are some ways to make your job more rewarding:

- Appreciate and celebrate your relationships with your clients and co-workers. Recognize the ways they are helping you. Be generous with your thanks. If you encounter dull or negative clients or co-workers, make it a game to find ways to enhance your connection. Compliment them, ask how their weekend was, and establish a frequency of passion by talking about what is uplifting to you. Discover where that person's passion lives. Someone who is numb or resistant is calling for love. If you can somehow deliver it, you will answer the unspoken request and you may see this person light up in your presence. Regardless of their response, you will have kept your soul alive.

- Adopt an attitude of play and lightheartedness in your work. Keep joy as your highest priority. Find ways to laugh when others are too serious. When you can joke about something, you have mastered the lesson it has come to teach you. Relieve tension with fun.

- Remember why you entered this career path. Reach to rekindle your original passion. You chose this journey for a reason. If you can get in touch with that reason, you can tap into the stream of joy, creativity, and productivity.

- Focus on the service you bring to your clients. You are making their lives better, the greatest reward of any profession. Shift your attention from "I'm not getting what I want" to "I am helping people get what they want." In that moment you will realize you *are* getting what you want, at the deepest level.

  I had the honor to meet Mr. Wahei Takeda, considered the "Warren Buffett of Japan." His wise business decisions have made him one of the wealthiest men in that country. I found Mr. Takeda to be an extraordinarily humble, approachable, and spiritual man. He is a marvelous example of someone with a great deal of money, who has kept his priorities in order. One of his business ventures is a cookie factory where he has trained all of the workers to cultivate an attitude of appreciation and blessing. When each person wraps a cookie, she says *arigato* ("thank you") and sends good wishes to the person who will eat it. As a result, the energy in the factory is vibrant and the business is hugely successful. When one of Mr. Takeda's employees has a baby, he gives the child a gold coin to stimulate prosperity in life. He took me on a tour of a personal museum he has created in his home to honor the gods and great leaders of Japan's history. Mr. Takeda has made his career a devotional journey and taught his employees how to do the same. He built his fortune on gratitude and service, and so can you.

- Use your mind productively, regardless of your task. If you have a job that does not require a lot of mental activity, such as that of a cleaner, assembly line worker, or laborer, use your time on your job to ponder your inspired visions. If you have a hobby you would like to turn into a career, mentally develop that project during your work hours. Nikola Tesla immigrated to the United States with the bold vision of turning Niagara Falls into a source of electricity. At first the only job he could get was that of ditch digger in New York City. Can you imagine—one of the greatest scientific geniuses of all time, relegated to digging ditches! But Tesla did not allow the position to daunt him. While digging, he was working out scientific inventions in his mind. By the time he got to a laboratory, the devices were complete in his vision. Tesla then connected with people who could finance his inventions, which proved to be the most transformational of the 20th century—including generating electricity from Niagara Falls. To this day we are trying to catch up with Tesla's genius and the inventions he didn't complete in his lifetime. So even his ditch-digging time was well spent.

A fellow who trims our yard is a retired military man in his 60s. When Tim's daughter was killed in an auto accident, he began to question why we are all here. He began to read books on spirituality and reincarnation. As I watched Tim tool around the lawn on his riding mower, I could see the wheels in his mind turning. When he finished, we shared profound metaphysical discussions. He told me, "I came to this amazing realization—I think we are really spiritual beings going through a material experience." I had to laugh because I, probably like you, have read and heard this famous idea from many authors and teachers. The innocence of Tim coming to this insight on his own tickled me. I was touched to see Tim use his time on the lawnmower to find some solace in the face of his loss and energize himself to lift his life.

Sometimes you can change your environment. Always you can change your mind. An attitudinal upgrade fulfills you in ways that exterior changes cannot.

- Start your workday or project on the right foot. Take a few moments to dedicate your endeavor to the most effective service, and establish your vision of your desired results. Meditate, visualize, pray, or say an affirmation that sets you up for your ideal experience. If you work with others of like mind, taking a few moments together to declare your shared intention will make a huge difference in the day or project, and significantly alter your results.

- Create an uplifting work environment. Post photos of your loved ones and role models, inspiring images, and motivational quotations. Vibrant plants, flowers, or a small fountain will purify the atmosphere. Decorate with colors and materials pleasing to you. Play your favorite music, if possible. Eliminate clutter, negative postings, noise, or disturbing music. Exercise your ability to create a positive work environment, and your investment will return many times over.

> ## THE MYTH:
> Your job is what it is.
>
> ## THE REALITY:
> Your job is what you make it.

## YOUR MONEY AND YOUR LIFE

Comedian Jack Benny had a reputation for being stingy with money. He capitalized on this personality quirk in comedy routines on his television show. Benny did a skit in which a mugger stuck a gun to his back and demanded, "Your money or your life." The camera zoomed in on Benny's face, contorted in confusion. As long silent moments ticked on, the audience roared with laughter. To a man obsessed with money, the choice between money and life posed a real dilemma!

Fortunately, we don't have to choose between money and life. We can have money *and* life. But we have to keep life first and let money come as an afterthought. As Stephen Covey advised, "The main thing is to keep the main thing the main thing." As I learned from Wahei Takeda, you can move lots of money around and stay connected to your spirit. The amount of money you move is less important than the consciousness with which you move it. Money lives in your mind more than in your bank account, so your mind is the place where you must upgrade your relationship with it. If you can move lots of money and still retain inner peace, you have mastered the world of finance.

## MANY DOORS OF PROVIDENCE

Don't get hung up dictating how your income should arrive. Providence can come through many doors. If you demand that sustenance come through a specified avenue, you may miss another avenue through which it is trying to reach you. Jenna wanted to pursue her passionate path of helping indigenous people. She made numerous trips to underdeveloped countries and bubbled with innovative ideas about how to improve their quality of life. Meanwhile, she was being supported by her mother, who sent her checks every month to help her pay her rent and other expenses. "I am afraid that I will have to get a job so I don't keep leaning on my mother's stipends," Jenna told me, dejected. "That will force me to cut back on my service work to indigenous people."

"You are missing a crucial link here," I told her.

"What's that?"

"The universe is already paying you to help the population you are serving," I explained. "That payment is coming through your mother. Has she complained about sending you regular checks?"

"No, I think she rather enjoys it."

"And does she have the money?"

"She has an inheritance from my father."

"So you are on Spirit's payroll, coming at the moment through your father's legacy and your mother's thoughtfulness. I suggest you accept it with humility and grace, and keep doing what fulfills your heart."

The inspiring documentary *The Wild Parrots of Telegraph Hill* chronicles the life of Mark Bittner, a gentle soul who for many years took care of a flock of wild parrots in San Francisco. Bittner spent most of his time feeding and caring for this large avian family, and did not do any jobs for pay for two and a half decades. During that period, people in the community recognized his service and he was given free rent, meals, and whatever else he needed. (As an interesting postscript, Bittner married the film's director, Judy Irving, whom he met while shooting the documentary. So he was provided for in relationship as well as his material needs.)

The system of divine compensation works in far broader strokes than we can see from the limited mind's perspective. There is not always a direct correspondence between the method by which you serve and the channel through which your compensation comes. Live in the grander picture and all of your needs will be taken care of by a hand larger than your own.

---

## THE MYTH:

Your financial sustenance must come through a particular job, person, or investment.

## THE REALITY:

You can be taken care of through an infinite number of ways. Providence knows how to find you.

---

## WHEN WORK GIVES WAY TO LIFE

If you have divided your world into two compartments, "work" and "life," you have missed the point of both. For most people, the idea of "work" implies toil, obligation, and even oppression. Yet only the ego experiences work. The spirit is established in joy. The ego manufactures the idea of work and then defines it as an enemy to be overcome. When you do what you love, your livelihood doesn't feel like work at all. Even challenges are exciting because they are part of a bigger, more rewarding game. When you stay true to authentic passion, resistance falls away. Real work/life balance is achieved when there is no more work to balance with life. There is only life.

---

## TRUTH #10
## YOU DO YOUR BEST WORK WHEN YOU ARE FULLY ALIVE

---

# EPILOGUE

Spirit means business because Spirit is your real business. That Spirit will tell you all you need to know to achieve all the material success you need. God withholds nothing. It is we who withhold from ourselves and each other. As you open to your true deservingness, prosperity will reach you with grace and ease. Life promises you enough because life *is* enough and created you *as* enough.

The universe does not want you to be poor or struggle for your good. Poverty at any level—financial, emotional, material, or in relationship—denies the nature of creation, which is unlimited abundance everywhere always. Life rejoices in you living in profuse riches, stemming from the riches of your soul. What you have or do not have in the material world is far less important than where your heart dwells. Live with a whole heart, and you will find fulfillment wherever you look.

The material world is the stage upon which you discover and express your true self. The purpose of your work is the same as the purpose of your life: to know your identity as an expression of a loving, creative God, and live it. Use your vocation to break the spell of oppressive beliefs that make work a prison, and choose instead beliefs that lead to freedom. When all is said and done, everything you can touch with your fingers will disappear and you will be left with your own dynamic reality.

You now have a new mission that goes beyond any you have adopted or assumed: You are to teach by example that business is a domain of connection, inspiration, service, and healing. Every interaction is an opportunity to deliver and receive blessing. If you engage in business for its own sake, you will feel empty and confused. When you dedicate your interactions to Higher Power, your soul will be satisfied and you will step naturally to higher ground.

The Power that created the entire universe is guiding you and will take you to every place you want and need to go. Trust it and use it. With God in you, behind you, through you, and around you, you cannot fail. The principles upon which the entire universe is founded are unfailing. They will sustain you and bless all that you do. This is the promise that will take you all the way home.

# ACKNOWLEDGMENTS

This book is the result of many years of learning to navigate the business world, a long and winding journey that helped me integrate my career path with my spiritual values. Proper acknowledgment would call me to thank and honor every single person and company I have ever done business with. Each has helped me discover what works and what does not work. Some insights I have gained by observing others, and others by recognizing the results of my attitudes and actions. Directly or indirectly, all have contributed to my life and my work.

It is, of course, impossible to cite all of these thousands of people and companies, so here I will just offer a broad and sincere blanket "Thank you for helping me learn, grow, and succeed." I wish you all success and prosperity on your own chosen path and, most of all, the peace of a satisfied soul.

More specifically, regarding this book, I must, as always, offer prime thanks to my beloved partner, Dee, who consistently supports me to bring forth ideas intended to make others' lives better. Dee and I have had countless discussions about how to wisely handle our business interactions and deal with people in a spirit of integrity, kindness, and service. She is my best sounding board, and together we somehow always arrive at visions and solutions that work.

I also honor Mr. Ken Honda, to whom this book is dedicated. Ken is a dear friend and a major force in establishing conscious commerce in Japan. Ken has always been extremely generous with his support for me, and serves as a rare and admirable model for merging immense goodheartedness with huge business success.

I must, as always, celebrate the extraordinary staff at Hay House, who work so efficiently and lovingly to bring you, the reader, the best quality material. My editor, Anne Barthel, is a person of deep graciousness and impeccable editorial skill, with whom I am honored to co-create. I also thank Sue Franco for her impeccable copyediting, Bryn Starr Best for the interior design, the Hay House art department, headed by Tricia Breidenthal, and especially Brad Foltz for the striking cover. My appreciation always embraces Reid Tracy, CEO, and Patty Gift, publisher. I am so blessed to work with you all.

I celebrate you, the reader, and any individual and company who seeks to infuse spiritual values into your vocation. *A Course in Miracles* tells us that whenever you offer any act of kindness, your act sends out ripples that touch and bless many people you may never know about. That is my prayer for this book, and for the book of your vocation and your life. I wish you brilliant success accompanied by a soaring soul.

# ABOUT THE AUTHOR

**Alan Cohen**, MA, holds degrees in psychology and human organizational development. He is the author of 27 popular inspirational books, including the bestselling *A Course in Miracles Made Easy* and the award-winning *A Deep Breath of Life*. He is a contributing writer for the #1 *New York Times* bestselling series *Chicken Soup for the Soul* and is featured in the book *101 Top Experts Who Help Us Improve Our Lives*. His books have been translated into 30 foreign languages.

A respected keynoter and seminar leader, Alan has taught at Montclair State College, Omega Institute for Holistic Studies and en*theos Academy for Optimal Living. He is a featured presenter in the award-winning documentary *Finding Joe*, celebrating the teachings of Joseph Campbell, as well as other inspirational videos.

Alan's radio show *Get Real* airs weekly on Hay House Radio, and his monthly column *From the Heart* is published in magazines internationally. His work has been presented on CNN and Oprah.com, and in *USA Today*, *The Washington Post*, and *The Huffington Post*.

Alan is the founder and director of the Foundation for Holistic Life Coaching. He also presents programmes on themes of life mastery, spiritual development and vision psychology – you will find many of these, plus DVDs, CDs, videos and online courses on his website.

He resides with his family in Hawaii.

**www.alancohen.com**

# LEARN MORE
# WITH ALAN COHEN

If you have enjoyed and benefited from *Spirit Means Business*, you may want to deepen your understanding and inspiration by participating in Alan Cohen's in-person seminars, online courses, life coach training, or online subscription programs.

**Quote for the Day**—An inspirational quotation e-mailed to you each day (free)

**Monthly e-Newsletter**—Uplifting articles and announcements of events (free)

**Wisdom for Today**—A stimulating life lesson e-mailed to you daily

**Live Webinars**—Interactive uplifting programs on topics relevant to spirituality, self-empowerment, and holistic living

**Online Courses**—In-depth experiential exploration of *Spirit Means Business*, relationships, prosperity, healing, prayer, metaphysics, and time management

**Life Coach Training**—Become a certified professional life coach or enhance your career and personal life with coaching skills

**Mastery Training**—A transformational retreat in Hawaii to align your life with your passion, power, and purpose

For information about all of these programs and new products and events, visit www.AlanCohen.com.

# HAY HOUSE TITLES OF RELATED INTEREST

YOU CAN HEAL YOUR LIFE, the movie, starring Louise Hay & Friends
(available as a 1-DVD program, an expanded 2-DVD set,
and an online streaming video)
Learn more at www.hayhouse.com/louise-movie

THE SHIFT, the movie, starring Dr. Wayne W. Dyer
(available as a 1-DVD program, an expanded 2-DVD set,
and an online streaming video)
Learn more at www.hayhouse.com/the-shift-movie

* * ▪ ▓    ▓ ▫ ▫ *

ABUNDANCE UNLEASHED: Open Yourself to More Money, Love,
Health, and Happiness Now, by Christian Mickelsen

BRING YOUR WHOLE SELF TO WORK: How Vulnerability Unlocks
Creativity, Connection, and Performance, by Mike Robbins

THE HAPPY HUMAN: Being Real in an Artificially Intelligent World,
by Gopi Kallayil

SUCCESS INTELLIGENCE: Essential Lessons and Practices from the World's
Leading Coaching Program on Authentic Success, by Robert Holden, Ph.D.

WORTHY: Boost Your Self-Worth to Grow Your Net Worth, by Nancy Levin

All of the above are available at www.hayhouse.co.uk.

# Hay House Podcasts
## Bring Fresh, Free Inspiration Each Week!

Hay House proudly offers a selection of life-changing
audio content via our most popular podcasts!

### Hay House Meditations Podcast

Features your favorite Hay House authors guiding you through meditations designed to help you relax and rejuvenate. Take their words into your soul and cruise through the week!

### Dr. Wayne W. Dyer Podcast

Discover the timeless wisdom of Dr. Wayne W. Dyer, world-renowned spiritual teacher and affectionately known as "the father of motivation." Each week brings some of the best selections from the 10-year span of Dr. Dyer's talk show on HayHouseRadio.com.

### Hay House World Summit Podcast

Over 1 million people from 217 countries and territories participate in the massive online event known as the Hay House World Summit. This podcast offers weekly mini-lessons from World Summits past as a taste of what you can hear during the annual event, which occurs each May.

### Hay House Radio Podcast

Listen to some of the best moments from HayHouseRadio.com, featuring expert authors such as Dr. Christiane Northrup, Anthony William, Caroline Myss, James Van Praagh, and Doreen Virtue discussing topics such as health, self-healing, motivation, spirituality, positive psychology, and personal development.

### Hay House Live Podcast

Enjoy a selection of insightful and inspiring lectures from Hay House Live, an exciting event series that features Hay House authors and leading experts in the fields of alternative health, nutrition, intuitive medicine, success, and more! Feel the electricity of our authors engaging with a live audience, and get motivated to live your best life possible!

Find Hay House podcasts on iTunes, or visit
www.HayHouse.com/podcasts for more info.

# HAY HOUSE
## *Look within*

Join the conversation about latest products, events, exclusive offers and more.

 Hay House UK

 @HayHouseUK

 @hayhouseuk

 healyourlife.com

# *We'd love to hear from you!*